The Freedmen's Bureau in South Carolina

1865-1872

The Freedmen's Bureau
in South Carolina

1865-1872

by Martin Abbott

THE UNIVERSITY OF NORTH CAROLINA PRESS · CHAPEL HILL

73773

To HELEN, GARY, *and* JUDITH

Each generation, it is said, rewrites its own history. Certainly this truism applies with particular force to the era of Reconstruction in American history. For a hundred years historians, writers, and partisans have searched for—and disagreed about— the nature and significance of the period. Within recent years a number of works have appeared which undertake sweeping revisions of established views, and several more are on the way. Partly, no doubt, this urge to reconsider Reconstruction has been prompted by the arrival of its centennial; the perspective of a century inevitably produces some qualification of older judgments. But mainly, one feels, it has come as a by-product of the continuing urgency of the debate over civil rights for the Negro, as the conscience of the nation has become more engaged in critical questions and vital issues which were first raised, and then left unanswered, by the events of that stormy postwar period. In more ways than one, in fact, the chief legacy of the era is to be found in the unsolved problem of race relations which it bequeathed to posterity for an answer.

Inevitably, much of the revived interest in Reconstruction has concerned itself with the Freedmen's Bureau, since it was this agency which faced the main challenge—and the greatest opportunity—of defining the meaning of freedom for four million bondsmen as they groped their way forth from slavery. Created by Congress in March of 1865, the Bureau would continue its major activities until the close of 1869, and some peripheral work until the end of 1872. During the three and a half years of its primary existence, it operated in all of the former slave states and, under the purpose of promoting the general welfare of the freedmen, came to be concerned with virtually every question affecting their future in a free society. The whole dimension of freedom, in fact, was conditioned by how nearly the agency fulfilled the purposes of its creation.

Yet the real test of the Bureau's worth is to be found not so much in the aims of Congress in creating it, or in the will of the national commissioner in directing it, but, rather, in how well or how feebly it met at the local level the actual needs of those whom it was designed to serve. As a human institution, its ultimate success or failure depended mainly upon the kind of response which its agents and officers in the field gave to the challenge before them—how much they gave in understanding, intelligence, tact, and resourcefulness to provide an answer to the complex question of what freedom had to offer the former bondsmen.

This study is an attempt to answer the question of the Bureau's response in South Carolina. It began years ago as a doctoral dissertation and has undergone extensive revision since then. My concern has been to show how, in this single state, Bureau officials in the counties and communities undertook to transform the aims of the agency into reality. I have also sought to consider the matter of whether, as has long been charged, these men used their office to further the cause of Radical Republicanism among the freedmen. Finally, I have raised some points about what might have been for the South, the Negro, and the nation if the actual achievements of the Bureau had more nearly matched the potential within it.

Like all those engaged in scholarly research, I have incurred many debts along the way. I am sincerely grateful to the staffs of all the libraries mentioned in the bibliography; they have given a uniform courtesy and kindness to my many requests of them. I should also like to thank the Shell Oil Assists Program whose grant to Oglethorpe College made possible a partial subsidy in support of publication of this work.

Finally, I wish to express a warm sense of gratitude to my former mentor at Emory University, Professor Bell I. Wiley. As a scholar and teacher he set me on the road to doing this work in its original form; as a friend and counselor over the years, he has maintained an active interest as I sought to develop new research and to recast the whole into a different form. I can only hope that the result might approach the standards of expectation he set for his graduate students and for himself.

Contents

The Freedmen's Bureau in South Carolina

1865-1872

Freedom for the slaves of the South came at different times and in different ways. As the Civil War progressed this "day of Jubilo" for many arrived with the appearance of Federal armies in their locality; for others it came during a moonless night when they could steal away in the search for its existence; and for those who remained faithfully at work on the land it came at war's end with the sober announcement by the owners that they were free. But however it developed, freedom for most would serve at first to be an exciting yet a strange and bewildering thing.

A child's delight, a brightness too huge to grasp,
The hidden nation, untaught, unrecognized,
Free at last, but not yet free with the free,
Ignorant, joyful, wronged, child-minded and searching,
Searching the army's road for this new wild thing
That means so much but can't be held in the hand,
That must be there, that yet is so hard to find,
This dream, this pentecost changing, this liberty.[1]

More personally, a former slave would recall in late life: "What I likes best, to be slave or free? Well, it's this way. In slavery I owns nothing and never owns nothing. In freedom I's own the home and raise the family. All that cause me worriment, and in slavery I has no worriment, but I takes the freedom."[2]

Actual freedom for many, and perhaps for most, did not come until the war had ended; constitutionally, it became a reality only with the ratification of the Thirteenth Amendment in December, 1865. But the commitment of the nation to the principle of freedom for all had been made in 1863 when President Lincoln had issued the Emancipation Proclamation, declaring the essential inconsistency of slavery with the American democratic creed. The Proclamation thus had answered one question, that of the

1. Stephen Vincent Benét, "John Brown's Body" in *Selected Works of Stephen Vincent Benét* (New York, 1942), I, 307.
2. B. A. Botkin, *Lay My Burden Down: A Folk History of Slavery* (Chicago, 1945), p. 267.

future of human bondage in America; but it had left unanswered another that was no less critical, that of the future place of the former bondsmen in a free society. Unless slavery had been what it was not, and could never be—a training school for citizenship—the four million Negroes still living under it in 1860 were bound to be ill-prepared for the challenge of freedom. As free men they would find new and bewildering obligations to be faced; new and different rights for which, as yet, they had neither the training nor the social experience. The transition which they must undergo was certain to be neither short nor painless. And unless they were given guidance, direction, encouragement, and aid, the promise of freedom might prove to be a deceptively cruel illusion.

Mindful of this, Congressmen who were concerned about the future of Negroes as free men began, even as the conflict continued, to turn their thoughts to the question of how best to secure that future. As early as December, 1863, Representative Thomas D. Eliot of Massachusetts introduced a bill to establish a Federal agency whose main responsibility would be that of guiding the ex-slaves along the path of freedom. But not until March 3, 1865, was such a measure finally enacted. It created within the War Department a Bureau of Refugees, Freedmen, and Abandoned Lands whose operations were to extend one year beyond the close of the war. Commonly called the Freedmen's Bureau, the agency was given the main task of promoting the general well-being of the freedmen and of white refugees. It was authorized to provide food, fuel, clothing, and medical care for the destitute of both groups, to make provisions for their education, and to make available, either for rent or for sale, abandoned lands within the South which were held by the Federal government. The President was empowered to appoint a commissioner who in turn could name as many as ten assistant commissioners to aid him. At the suggestion of Secretary of War Edwin M. Stanton, Lincoln finally decided to fill the post of commissioner with General O. O. Howard, a veteran Civil War commander of sincere if rather conspicuous Christian principles. His wartime experience had carried him from Fair Oaks and Chancellorsville to Gettysburg, Chattanooga, and Atlanta. And then, from the summer of 1864 until the close of the conflict, he commanded the Army of the Tennessee as it marched with

Sherman through Georgia and on northward into the Carolinas. On April 26, 1865, he became commissioner of the Bureau by order of President Andrew Johnson, who acted to carry out the intention of Lincoln in the matter.[3]

Though the naming of a director for the Bureau thus awaited the close of the conflict, the question of the freed Negro and his future role in Southern society had begun to demand an answer much earlier, as fugitive slaves in growing numbers found their way into Union lines. And nowhere did it grow so acute so early as along the coast of South Carolina. There, when Federal forces captured Port Royal, Beaufort, and the neighboring sea islands in late 1861, they found thousands of slaves left behind by their fleeing owners. Almost immediately Secretary of the Treasury Salmon P. Chase, who for years had been a leading abolitionist and who now hoped that the war might serve as the occasion for emancipation, sent a personal representative to study the situation and report to him. The agent, E. L. Pierce, following his investigation, proposed a plan for looking after the "contrabands" until more permanent arrangements might be made by Congress. With the approval of Chase, he proceeded to recruit the needed personnel and to launch the "Sea Island Experiment" in March of 1862.[4]

Pierce's program sought to promote the welfare of the sea island Negroes by naming superintendents who would organize their labor on the plantation and establish schools for their education. Under the supervision of some forty white superintendents, the Negroes were set to work cultivating the abandoned plantations at a standard wage of forty cents a day and rations. If all went well, Pierce believed, enough cotton could be grown to repay the Federal Treasury for whatever expense it had incurred in supporting the enterprise. In the field of education

3. The story of the background and beginnings of the Bureau can be found in George R. Bentley, *A History of the Freedmen's Bureau* (Philadelphia, 1955), Chaps. I-IV. See also John A. Carpenter, *Sword and Olive Branch: Oliver Otis Howard* (Pittsburgh, 1964).

4. The account which follows of the Sea Island Experiment is based mainly on Guion G. Johnson, *A Social History of the Sea Islands* (Chapel Hill, 1930), and E. L. Pierce, "The Freedmen at Port Royal," *Atlantic Monthly*, XII (1863), 291-315. See also Willie L. Rose, *Rehearsal for Reconstruction: The Port Royal Experiment* (Indianapolis, 1964), a brilliant account of the enterprise which appeared too late to be fully incorporated into this study.

two private Northern groups, the Educational Commission of Boston and the Freedman's Relief Association of New York, gave extensive help through recruiting and paying the teachers who were needed for the schools. By the middle of June, 1862, about nine thousand Negroes on the sea islands were involved in the experiment.

In the summer the entire project was transferred from the Treasury to the War Department and placed under the direction of General Rufus Saxton, who soon introduced some changes in the original plan. Under his direction, all of the area seized by Federal troops was divided into three large districts, with a general supervisor over each; the districts were then subdivided, with local superintendents in immediate charge of one or more plantations. Each plantation was marked off into a number of plots and leased, rent-free, to the Negro families, though each laborer was required to work a certain amount of time in government-operated cotton fields. The national government supplied provisions and a wage of twenty-five cents a day to each worker, expecting to be reimbursed for its expenses from the proceeds of the cotton crop.

Saxton also hoped to strengthen the program of education by placing at least one teacher on every plantation. His goal was not realized fully, but by 1864 thirty schools were in operation with a staff of about forty-five teachers and an enrollment of two thousand students. Whether or not the kind of schooling offered was really effective is open to question. The teachers, of course, were without experience in working with ex-slaves and, in any case, were prepared neither by background nor by training to offer a program of studies any better suited to the needs of a people just emerging from bondage. Thus, they taught what they knew: the classics, geography, rhetoric, and arithmetic, none of which served the immediate and pressing question before the emancipated Negro of how to sustain himself as a free man in a free society.

Another characteristic of the educational enterprise was the evangelical fervor which accompanied it; many if not most of the teachers, viewing themselves as laborers in the Lord's vineyard, came as much to declare the truth of religion as to spread the light of learning.[5] The whole undertaking, no doubt, was conditioned by Saxton's own religious zeal whose mood was typically expressed by him in his Thanksgiving Proclamation of 1862: "You, Freemen and women, have never before had such cause for thankfulness. Your simple faith has been vindicated. . . . Your chains are broken. Your days of bondage and mourning are ended, and you are forever free. If you cannot yet see your way clear in the future, fear not; put your trust in the Lord, and he will vouchsafe, as did he to the Israelites of old, the cloud by day and the pillar of fire by night, to guide your footsteps 'through the wilderness' to the promised land."[6]

Yet whatever the question as to the effectiveness of the educational efforts, the former slaves doubtless learned some valuable lessons about industry and thrift. Saxton reported in early 1865 that during the two and a half years of his administration the Negroes had grown about $300,000 worth of cotton, purchased a number of plots of land offered for sale by the government, and deposited almost $250,000 in a Freedman's Savings Bank founded by him less than a year before. If it demonstrated nothing more, the Sea Island Experiment was providing impressive evidence that the freed slave was able to sustain himself outside the framework of slavery.[7]

Early in 1865 the entire project underwent a basic change when General William T. Sherman and his army arrived on the Georgia coast, following their famous March to the Sea. As they had swept through the states and then turned northward toward the Carolinas, large numbers of slaves, seeking the fabled liberty, had swarmed to join the moving military columns. Wishing to rid himself of this encumbrance without at the same time inflicting injury upon the Negroes, Sherman conferred with

5. The best account of the whole educational endeavor in the South is in Henry L. Swint, *The Northern Teacher in the South* (Nashville, 1941).

6. Ray A. Billington (ed.), *The Journal of Charlotte L. Forten* (New York, 1953), p. 234.

7. Rufus Saxton to O. O. Howard, August 15, 1865, Vol. 9, records of the Bureau of Refugees, Freedmen, and Abandoned Lands. These voluminous records in the National Archives, Washington, D. C., are divided into two broad categories: those relating to Howard's office in Washington, and those pertaining to the individual states where the Bureau operated. Hereafter, the designation "Bureau Records" will be used to indicate that the manuscript is from the records of the central office; "Bureau Records, S. C.," to identify items in the records for South Carolina.

Secretary of War Stanton and some twenty Negro spokesmen about the problem. He then issued Special Field Order No. 15, setting aside all of the sea islands from Charleston south, not already disposed of, and all of the abandoned rice fields along the rivers for a distance of thirty miles inland. In these areas Negroes were to be settled and assigned "possessory titles" to not more than forty acres per family until Congress should provide a permanent solution. General Saxton, with the title of Inspector of Settlements and Plantations, was named to supervise the implementation of the order.[8]

Saxton moved with decision in taking possession of about three hundred thousand acres of land and settling some forty thousand freedmen on them. Through a series of speeches and circulars he informed both races of the changes to be introduced. To the whites he announced that thirty days would be allowed for them to vacate any lands held in violation of Sherman's order, after which violators were to be arrested.[9] To the Negroes he declared in a speech: "I came to tell you to get the land. I wish every colored man, every head of a family in this department to acquire a freehold, a little home that he can call his own."[10] In response the Negroes, despite the fact that the growing season was well advanced, went to work with a will, not only to cultivate the soil but also in other ways to prove themselves worthy of the boon of freedom. "On some of the islands," wrote Saxton, "the freedmen have established civil government with constitution and laws, for the regulation of their entire affairs, with all the different departments of Schools, Churches, building roads and other improvements."[11] The Sea Island Experiment, modified and strengthened by Sherman's order, ceased to be an experiment and came instead to be a successful venture—a success for which Saxton, as its director for almost three years, could take much of the credit.

Upon the close of the war Saxton found the scope of his duties considerably enlarged with his appointment in June, 1865,

8. *War of the Rebellion: A Compilation of the Official Records of the Union and Confederate Armies* (Washington, 1880-1901), series 1, XLVII, part 2, 60-62.

9. Circular, April 22, 1865, in the South Caroliniana Library, University of South Carolina.

10. Charleston *Courier,* May 13, 1865.

11. Saxton to Howard, December 6, 1865, Bureau Records, Box 732.

as one of the assistant commissioners of the newly created Freedmen's Bureau. Though originally named to direct the activities of the agency in South Carolina, Georgia, and Florida, he gave his main energy and attention throughout to affairs in South Carolina. And since, in time, General Howard named other men to superintend Bureau business in the other two states, it may be said that Saxton's career with the agency was, for all practical purposes, confined to this one state.

The position of assistant commissioner carried with it a heavy responsibility, since by law of Congress the Bureau was charged with the broad duties of promoting the social, economic, and educational well-being of the emancipated slaves. In light of the fact that the Bureau was created within the War Department and, further, that Bureau officers were expected to co-operate with the military in administering affairs in the postwar South, Saxton appeared to be an ideal choice for the new post to which he was assigned. A native of Massachusetts and a graduate of West Point, he had served in various army posts in the West between 1849 and the outbreak of the Civil War. Until he was named in 1862 to direct the Sea Island Experiment, he had a brief taste of military campaigning in western Virginia and then in the Union expedition sent late in 1861 to capture Port Royal on the Carolina coast.[12]

Though not identified with the abolitionists before the war, he nevertheless brought to his Bureau office much of their moral fervor and emotional intensity. The essence of his character was captured by Whitelaw Reid, a journalist touring the South in 1865, who described him as a handsome man with "black hair and luxurious English whiskers" and then observed: "He looks . . . narrow, but intense; not very profound in seeing the right, but energetic in doing it when seen. . . ."[13] He was undoubtedly sincere in his concern for the future well-being of the freed slaves; yet his fervent emotionalism about them, and his naïve notion that the complex problems before them had simple answers, caused him to substitute feeling for realism in his efforts to find meaningful solutions. Negro and white, he believed,

12. *Appleton's Cyclopedia of American Biography* (New York, 1887-1889), V, p. 410; Saxton to Howard, June 4, 1865, Bureau Records, Box 728.

13. Whitelaw Reid, *After the War: A Southern Tour* (New York, 1866), p. 80.

needed only to be taught to forget two hundred years of master-slave relationship. He also had a talent for bombast which regularly manifested itself in his proclamations and speeches. His first circular after becoming assistant commissioner was typical: "The freedmen should accept with thankful hearts the great boon of liberty which a kind Providence has vouchsafed them" while the late masters "should heed the great struggle through which the nation has passed and accept the result as the verdict of the Almighty against human slavery." He added in conclusion: "Adopting the noble creed of our late honored President, 'with malice towards none and charity to all, with firmness in the right as God gives us to see the right,' let us strive earnestly to establish peace and good will; and . . . do what we can to inaugurate for our country a fairer future of happiness and prosperity."[14] Saxton could also demonstrate a certain guilelessness in advising the freedmen, most of whom had spent all of their lives tilling the soil: "After being sure you have planted sufficient corn and potatoes for food then put in all the cotton and rice you can. . . . Bear in mind that cotton is a regal plant, and the more carefully it is cultivated, the greater will be the crop."[15]

But in at least one regard Saxton was a greater realist than most of his contemporaries. He believed that if the Bureau were to be really effective, its life must be extended further than the original limit of one year beyond the close of the war. Accordingly, in response to a request from Howard in November, 1865, he submitted a proposed bill for prolonging the life of the agency and, at the same time, considerably broadening its powers. Besides incorporating all the features of the original act, the proposal added several new clauses relating to Southern lands acquired by the Federal government through confiscation, seizure, or other means. In creating the Bureau and placing under its control all such lands for the benefit of freedmen and refugees, Congress had declared that the titles granted to purchasers and tenants would be "such as the United States can convey," an

14. Circular #1, June 10, 1865, Bureau Records, S. C., Box 496. Saxton was also a rather careless administrator. His successor, Robert K. Scott, found so few papers from Saxton's regime that he had to request agents to provide him with copies of the orders assigning them to duty. Bentley, *Freedmen's Bureau,* p. 138.

15. Circular #2, August 16, 1865, Bureau Records, S. C., Box 496.

ambiguous phrase suggesting legal uncertainty. To remove all doubt in this matter Saxton's proposed bill called for the Federal government to grant clear and unconditional deeds to all those who rented or purchased lands seized by Federal authority. It also called for a broad extension of Bureau authority through authorizing the assistant commissioner to employ two agents for each county within the state, and through arming all Bureau officials with sweeping power to arrest and bring to trial all persons interfering with their legitimate operations. Moreover, the assistant commissioner was to be clothed with authority to set aside the actions of any civil or provost court which, in his opinion, failed to recognize the rights and liberties of freedmen, and neither the military nor any other authorities were to have any right "to interfere with the action of the Assistant Commissioner of this bureau." Because of what he termed widespread disloyalty that still prevailed among the whites, Saxton further proposed that Federal troops should be stationed at every point deemed necessary by an agent, such regiments to consist of native Negroes under the command of white officers.[16]

Such a proposal, to say the least, was too sweeping to win acceptance by the public of the day or to secure any substantial support in Congress. Yet unrealistic as it was in one sense, in another Saxton's proposed measure clearly recognized the central problem of the Bureau: insufficient means for doing the work expected of it. From the beginning the agency in South Carolina faced formidable problems which Saxton and his subordinates, with the means available, could not solve. There was, for one thing, the inevitable chaos and confusion of war, especially in the field of agriculture. Many of the farms and plantations had suffered from devastation, neglect, and abandonment; tools, implements, and seed were scarce; hundreds of war-weary landowners were returning without money or means to face the bleakness of the times; and thousands of freedmen had become physically displaced and emotionally disoriented during the conflict and its aftermath.

Such problems as these, in themselves, would have challenged the resources of the Bureau; yet by no means were they the only ones facing the agency. Another was the shortage of funds. Congress, in creating the Bureau, had neglected to appropriate

16. Saxton to Howard, June 7, 1865, Bureau Records, Box 728.

any money for its use, believing that it could realize an adequate income from the sale and rental of Southern lands seized by Federal authority during and after the war. And this initially appeared to be the case, especially in South Carolina, where the Bureau expected to have the proceeds from the sale of cotton grown during the Sea Island Experiment as well as from the sale and rental of three hundred thousand acres of abandoned and confiscated land.

But this expectation soon proved false. Proceeds from the sea island cotton, amounting to about $300,000, went to the Treasury Department instead of the Bureau, in spite of the protests of General Saxton.[17] A similar disappointment soon developed about income from confiscated and abandoned lands. Because he was strongly opposed to any wholesale expropriation of Southern property, President Johnson in September of 1865 ordered the return of all lands to their former owners whenever such persons had complied with the presidential program of pardon for ex-Confederates. The only exception consisted of those lands already sold under court order.[18] Though entirely out of sympathy with the presidential policy, Saxton had little choice but to carry it out. By the end of the year he reported with discouragement that of the three hundred thousand acres of land and the twelve hundred houses once controlled by the Bureau in South Carolina, the majority of both had been returned to their former owners.[19] The effect of this development can be seen in what happened to the Bureau's finances. Late in 1865 its rental income amounted to $6,000 per month; a year later, to only $50 a month.[20] The inevitable result was a sharp curtailment in its program at a time when the need for its assistance among the people was greatest.

Inevitably, too, Saxton was compelled to make cutbacks in the size of his personnel force. He had to discharge most civilian agents in the field and to seek, instead, to have more army officers assigned by Union military commanders in the state to service with the Bureau, a procedure authorized by the congressional act of creation. But the results were far from satis-

17. Saxton to Howard, August 15, 1865, Bureau Records, S. C., Vol. 9.
18. The complete story of the land question is related in Chap. IV of this study.
19. Saxton to Howard, December 6, 1865, Bureau Records, Box 732.
20. Bentley, *Freedmen's Bureau*, p. 74.

factory. Many officers were unsympathetic with the work of the agency and still others resented the additional work they were expected to do without additional pay. Consequently, the Bureau came to be staffed largely by men who shared little of Saxton's fervent idealism or bright hopes about the freed slaves. Initially, at least, General Q. A. Gillmore, commander of the Federal forces in the state, displayed a co-operative attitude, promising Saxton that he would direct every sub-district and post commander to act as the Bureau's representative in localities where there was none.[21] Yet not even this action could supply the needed personnel. Two months after becoming assistant commissioner, Saxton reported that his entire force for dispersal over the state's thirty-one counties numbered only seventeen. To care for the whole upstate area westward from Columbia to the mountains—a large region containing thirteen counties—were but five officers, three of whom were at the capital of Columbia, one at Anderson, and one at Newberry. Even at the close of 1865, six months after assuming office, Saxton had only twenty-four assistants and twenty doctors to look after the interests of the four hundred thousand freedmen in the state.[22]

During the same time military officials grew progressively more indifferent towards Saxton's many requests for help. Despite early promises of co-operation, General Gillmore refused with increasing frequency to assign officers to duty with the Bureau by replying curtly to Saxton's appeals, "The interests of the service will not permit the detailing of officers from their regiments." To make his position more emphatic the commander in late October issued an order that no subordinate officer in the entire military department had the right to assign men to Bureau service; all such directives, he added, must come from departmental headquarters.[23] With financial means dwindling and co-operation from the military forces uncertain, Saxton faced mounting difficulty in securing the personnel he needed. By the end of 1865 there were many counties in which no Bureau official resided, and others in which agents were too few to do the job. A typical situation was that in Georgetown county,

21. Gillmore to Saxton, August 10, 1865, Bureau Records, Box 728-A.
22. Report, December 17, 1865, Bureau Records, among the unclassified and unboxed materials.
23. Correspondence between Saxton and Gillmore, October 25-26, 1865, Bureau Records, S. C., Box 473.

where only one officer and seven enlisted men were stationed to look after the needs of some twenty to twenty-five thousand Negroes.[24]

Another problem that confronted Saxton was the active opposition that developed among some military officers towards the work of the Bureau. From Orangeburg, for example, a Bureau agent complained that the military commander there was wholly disinclined to recognize his authority. "Permit me to add," he declared, ". . . that if a spirit of actual hostility to the Freedmen's Bureau does not exist in the Dist. . . . , there is manifestly a lack of that co-operation essential to a successful prosecution of the work. I am forced to believe, that much of the prejudice, apparent among every subordinate commander to what is derisively termed 'negro equality' is largely the echo from Dist. Head Qr. at Charleston."[25] From an agent in Beaufort came a similar complaint about the refusal of the commander there to acknowledge the Bureau's authority and a further charge that military courts were guilty of flagrant injustice towards the freedmen.[26]

Still another turn of events that hampered the Bureau's work developed in the area of relief for the destitute. Though without an appropriation for such work, the Bureau, nevertheless, had been able initially to provide a great deal of assistance to the needy under its authorization to call upon the military establishment for the supplies of food, clothing, and medicine needed to relieve destitution among Negroes and white refugees. Until the fall of 1865 Bureau officials had encountered little difficulty in getting the necessary supplies; but gradually they came to find a growing unwillingness by military authorities to issue the provisions requested. The director of a freedmen's hospital at Beaufort, for example, reported that he had been compelled to discharge all patients and to refuse admittance to any new ones because the local commissary commander suddenly refused to issue any more rations for the use of the institution.[27] And in

24. A. J. Willard to Saxton, November 13, 1865, Bureau Records, S. C., Vol. 191.

25. William F. Young to Saxton, July 10, 1865, Bureau Records, S. C., Box 473.

26. H. G. Judd to Saxton, November 20, 1865, Bureau Records, S. C., Box 472.

27. A. J. Wakefield to W. R. De Witt, September 25, 1865, Bureau Records, S. C., Box 473.

November General Gillmore halted the issue of provisions to white refugees. Personal appeals from Saxton proved futile. After vainly requesting Gillmore to reconsider his decision, the assistant commissioner then informed Bureau headquarters in Washington of the impasse. Ultimately the matter was turned over to the War Department, which ruled that withholding of rations was unwarranted and went on to assure Bureau officials that Gillmore's newly-named successor, General D. E. Sickles, would prove more co-operative.[28]

But the hopes raised by such a ruling soon proved false. Sickles also refused to authorize the issuing of provisions to the Bureau for any group except destitute freedmen. Moreover, his subordinates throughout the state often reserved to themselves the right to judge the merits of need, irrespective of the Bureau's recommendations.[29] In the Beaufort area, for example, the military commander established a board to meet once a month to examine all applicants for relief and to confine strictly the issue of rations to the needy. The result, according to an officer of the Bureau on an inspection tour, was widespread suffering among many who were destitute but who were unable to appear before the examining board. Protests by the local Bureau agent were disregarded by the military authorities.[30] Similar developments occurred elsewhere within the state, causing the Bureau's program of relief to fall far short of the need in postwar South Carolina.

By the end of 1865, in the field of relief as well as in most other areas of its responsibility, the Bureau was hobbling rather than striding along towards its goal of organizing freedom for the emancipated slaves. Undeniably it had accomplished something worthwhile in bringing some relief to the suffering, in helping the dislocated to return to their homes, and in establishing an educational program for the benefit of the freedmen. But the achievement measured only meagerly against the need. The bright hope and the fervent idealism of the early days had progressively lost their glow. Saxton himself became deeply dispirited, especially

28. H. W. Smith to Saxton, November 1, 1865, Bureau Records, S. C., Box 473.
29. Saxton to Sickles, December 6, 1865, Bureau Records, S. C., Vol. 10.
30. C. H. Howard to O. O. Howard, December 30, 1865, *Senate Executive Documents*, 39 Cong., 1 Sess., no. 27 (serial 1238), pp. 123-34.

after the presidential order restoring the sea island lands to their white owners.

Moreover, he had incurred the President's displeasure through his reluctance to carry out that order, a fact which resulted in his removal as assistant commissioner in January, 1866.[31] Though he carried with him the deep and almost reverent love of the Negroes who had known him,[32] he left office with a heavy heart, keenly conscious of what had been left undone. By no means were all of the Bureau's difficulties of his own making. Some were the inevitable by-products of war; others were caused by circumstances beyond his control. Yet in some ways the difficulties were compounded, rather than simplified, by his own unrealistic beliefs. Failing to recognize that racial adjustment between black and white in postwar South Carolina was a complex matter of many dimensions, he developed an approach that, while commendable in its commitment and sincerity, was deplorably naïve. His idealism, thus misdirected, proved to be as much a source of weakness as of strength.

31. The order of reassignment read that Saxton was being relieved "at his own request." War Department, Special Order #12, January 22, 1866, Bureau Records, S. C., Box 476. But in fact he was removed at the insistence of Johnson, who had made slight effort to conceal his displeasure over Saxton's opposition to the presidential program of restoration. C. H. Howard to O. O. Howard, December 6, 1865, and Saxton to O. O. Howard, December 4, 1865, O. O. Howard Papers, Bowdoin College Library.

32. Just prior to his departure from Charleston, the freedmen of the city held a mass meeting to honor him for his labors in their behalf. The assembly presented him with a number of gifts and adopted several resolutions highly laudatory of his work as assistant commissioner. *South Carolina Leader*, January 22, 1866.

The beginning of the new year is traditionally a time of optimistic hope and good cheer about the future. But in January of 1866 Robert K. Scott, as newly-named assistant commissioner for South Carolina, must have found little that inspired either optimism or cheer. As yet but half-formed, the Bureau was woefully undermanned and critically underfinanced. It was also hampered by uncertainty about how much longer it was to exist, since the act of creation had defined its duration as one year beyond the close of the war. Moreover, military commanders, without whose co-operation the Bureau could scarcely function in carrying out its work, had grown refractory and many army officers resentful over assignment to service with the agency.

Scott must have felt a further discouragement when he viewed the lingering dislocations of war throughout the state, for the ravages of wartime were still much in evidence. This was especially true in the realm of agriculture, a pursuit vital to the welfare of white and black alike. The barren farm conditions were all too evident in the decaying plantations, overgrown fields, sagging buildings, rotting fences, and scrawny livestock.[1] And to the problem of economic instability was added that of social disorder created by a widespread restlessness that gripped large numbers of Negroes during 1865 and early 1866. Sidney Andrews, a responsible Northern journalist who visited the state a few months after the war's end, commented upon the phenomenon. Swarms of freedmen were in motion, especially towards the coast, where many expected to find free land given by the government—a notion which Andrews described as the source "of much idleness and discontent." Some believed that all whites were going to be removed from the entire lower part of the state in order to permit wholesale resettlement of Negroes; others were on the move from a vague feeling about Charleston's being a

1. Francis B. Simkins and Robert H. Woody, *South Carolina During Reconstruction* (Chapel Hill, 1932), Chap. VIII.

haven and home; and still others were going out, "ignorantly and mistakenly, yet seeking nothing less noble and worthy than freedom." Andrews' judgment, perhaps overstated since his observations were confined to the coastal region, was that the entire labor system was "in an utterly demoralized condition."[2]

In surveying the work before the Bureau, Scott thus faced a task both complex and challenging. But if he felt misgivings he did not betray them, a fact explained perhaps by the considerable experience he had gathered in adapting to new situations. A native of Pennsylvania who had been reared in Ohio, he had attended Central College and then a medical school before succumbing to the California gold fever. Traveling there in 1850, he had pursued mining and medical practice with indifferent success and then undertaken a prospecting tour in South America. At length he had returned to his hometown of Napoleon, Ohio, where he managed to become a man of some means through his practice of medicine and his dealing in real estate. Upon the outbreak of the Civil War he organized a regiment of volunteers, saw extensive battle service that included the campaigns of Fort Donelson, Shiloh, Vicksburg, and Atlanta, and rose ultimately to the rank of major general. Named as assistant commissioner of the Bureau for South Carolina in 1866, he held that position until he was elected to the governorship of the state in 1868 and re-elected in 1870. He returned at length to Ohio where, until his death in 1900, he developed his real estate interests.[3]

Though his background may not have suggested it, Scott from the very beginning was more realistic in his attitude about the Bureau and its work than had been Rufus Saxton. Unlike his predecessor he recognized that whites of South Carolina were incapable of adjusting overnight to the social revolution produced by the freeing of the slaves; and though steadfast in his determination to safeguard the rights of the freedmen, he was no less determined to avoid needless offense towards the whites through gratuituous reminders to them of the changed reality. Aware that the Bureau was scheduled for only a brief existence,

2. Sidney Andrews, *The South Since the War* (Boston, 1866), pp. 96-100, *passim*.
3. Toledo *Blade*, August 13, 1900; Napoleon (Ohio) *Democratic Northwest*, August 16, 1900.

and that long after it had gone the freedmen must go on living among the whites, he hoped that agency might achieve its goals without fostering ill-will between the two races. He reminded his subordinates that while "the end and aim of the Bureau is to secure the freed people protection in their natural and acquired rights, . . . in securing that end it is not necessary that injustice to white citizens . . . be used as a means." Repeatedly and consistently he supplemented words with deeds by dispensing an even-handed justice; if on the one hand he could threaten whites with seizure of their lands and crops for violating labor agreements with their Negro workers, on the other he could also make clear his determination to compel the freedmen to fulfill their obligations under such agreements.[4]

Like Saxton, Scott from the outset was seriously hampered in his work by the shortage of personnel. Through some help from military commanders in assigning officers to Bureau service and by hiring a few civilian agents with the limited funds available, he did manage during his first month in office to develop a total field force of sixty-one officers and agents—an improvement upon the force of forty-four reported by Saxton in the preceding December, but one still too small to do the job needed throughout the state.[5] Yet hardly had Scott dispersed these subordinates before he was compelled by a growing shortage of money to discharge thirty of the thirty-one civilians on his personnel roster.[6] A typical situation which resulted was that in the area of the state's capital of Columbia, where the Bureau had but three officials to look after affairs in a large region of seven counties.[7] A similar situation prevailed in another district where the officer in charge reported that in supervising affairs in six counties, embracing forty-seven thousand square miles and containing about fifty thousand freedmen, he had no assistants at all. Upon his arrival, he said, he had found troop garrisons in four places, providing him with some means of enforcing his authority; but re-

4. Scott to James L. Orr, December 13, 1866, MS, S. C. Historical Commission; Scott to A. P. Carahar, August 11, 1866; Scott to Edward Fowler, November 1, 1866; and Scott to D. T. Corbin, March 28, 1866, Bureau Records, S. C., Vol. 11; Fairfield *Herald*, April 17, 1867.

5. Roster of Officers and Civilians, January, 1866, Bureau Records, S. C., Box 484.

6. *Ibid.*

7. W. J. Harkisheimer to Scott, June 27, 1866, Bureau Records, S. C., Vol. 132.

cently, he continued, three of those had been withdrawn, leaving only a token force for his use.[8] Under such circumstances as these—more typical than untypical in the spring of 1866—it is an unhappy yet an unmistakably clear fact that there were several counties of the state in which, a full year after the Bureau had begun to operate, the freedmen had never seen or felt its presence.

But relief and partial remedy in the matter came during the summer of 1866 when Congress, over the veto of the President, passed a bill prolonging the life of the Bureau for two additional years and appropriating almost $7,000,000 for its use.[9] With a stable allotment of funds available Scott was able for the first time to put into the field a force that at least was more than token in size. By October of that year he listed a total complement of thirty-one clerks and laborers whose monthly wages ranged between $6 and $125; two agents, whose average monthly salary was $125; seventeen private physicians under contract at $100 a month for medical care to destitute freedmen; and twenty-seven reserve army officers in addition to five regular army officers. Including Scott's headquarters staff, the total Bureau force numbered eighty-seven, of whom fifty-one were actively engaged in service in the field. By the middle of 1867 the total force had increased somewhat to eighty-eight, of whom forty were agents and officers in the field, eight members of the headquarters in Charleston, eighteen physicians under contract to the agency, and the remainder clerks and laborers.[10]

Neither before nor after this time was the Bureau in South Carolina as strong in manpower resources. Yet even at this peak of its strength its force was still woefully inadequate to realize its

8. G. W. Gile to Scott, May 18, 1866, Bureau Records, S. C., Vol. 175.

9. George R. Bentley, A History of the Freedmen's Bureau (Philadelphia, 1955), Chap. IX.

10. Roster of Officers and Civilians, October, 1866, Bureau Records, S. C., Box 484, and Roster of Officers and Civilians, July, 1867, ibid., Box 485.

The pattern of organization as finally evolved provided for the grouping of counties in the state into districts and sub-districts; officers in charge of a district were designated as acting assistant commissioners, those over a sub-district as sub-assistant commissioners, and officers or civilians within a sub-district as agents. Circular letter from Scott, February 19, 1867, Bureau Records, S. C., Vol. 26.

purposes. Two instances from the period might be cited to il-
lustrate the truth of the matter. In the coastal district of Colleton
were but one officer and one agent to attend to the affairs of
forty thousand freedmen; they had no help at all except that
given by six contract physicians whose concern, on a part-time
basis, was solely with the physical health of the Negroes.[11] At
the opposite end of the state, in the foothills of the mountains,
another Bureau official confronted a similar situation. Responsible for three counties with an area of three thousand square miles
and thirty thousand freedmen, this officer had a small garrison
of troops at his disposal for a few months, but generally was
without any assistance in looking after his responsibilities.[12] Nor
are these instances exceptional. From all parts of the state officers
and agents told of the impossibility of discharging their complex
duties with the inadequate means at hand. Washington might
proclaim, and the assistant commissioner might direct, but
neither of these would put into the counties, towns, and communities the number of men needed to give practical and meaningful supervision to the needs and wants of the freedmen in
seeking a liberty of substance.

And the problem of personnel grew greater with the passing
of time. By the end of 1867 Scott had reduced somewhat the size
of his force in anticipation of the scheduled end of the Bureau's
life during the following summer. Moreover, during 1868 the
Veterans Reserve Corps was discontinued, thereby depriving the
Bureau of those reserve officers who had served with the agency
from the beginning. As a result the Bureau's staff was seriously
reduced, since money was not available for hiring civilian re-
placements.[13] Furthermore, Scott resigned in the summer of
1868, following his election to the governorship of the state, an
event which further circumscribed the Bureau's effectiveness,
since his experienced ability as assistant commissioner was ir-
replaceable.[14]

11. Roster of Officers and Civilians, July, 1867, Bureau Records, S. C.,
Box 485.
12. John W. De Forest, A Union Officer in the Reconstruction (New
Haven, 1948), p. xxix.
13. Scott to the four military post commanders, December 19, 1867, and
Scott to Howard, November 29, 1867, Bureau Records, S. C., Vol. 12.
14. War Department, Special Order #162, July 9, 1868, Bureau Records,
S. C., Vol. 11.

In spite of such reverses, the agency continued to hobble along for some time. Under additional legislation of Congress its entire operation was prolonged in certain states, including South Carolina, until the middle of 1869, and its work in education and assistance to colored veterans everywhere continued for three additional years.[15] Under the direction of Colonel John R. Edie, Scott's successor, the force of the Bureau was steadily reduced to conform to the cutback in funds and operations until by the beginning of 1869 total personnel numbered only nine. In May of that year Edie was succeeded by Horace Neide, who served mainly as caretaker until the virtual disbandment of the Bureau at the end of the month. At that time the office of assistant commissioner was discontinued, the director thereafter being designated simply as superintendent of education; all but a handful of officers, agents, and clerks were discharged; and the bulk of Bureau property was sold at auction. In July Neide was succeeded as superintendent of education by Major Edward L. Deane, who served until June, 1870, when the office was abolished for want of funds.[16] Two aspects of the Bureau's work continued for two years longer: that of helping Negro veterans in filing certain claims, and that of trying to collect payment for supplies advanced by the Bureau to farmers and planters on crop-lien securities during earlier years. At last, on June 30, 1872, the agency was formally disbanded by law of Congress, and all unfinished business transferred to the office of the Assistant Adjutant General of the Army.[17]

The seven years of its whole existence had been, in terms of achievement, years neither of famine nor of plenty. The Bureau had planted and tilled and harvested, though its planting had occasionally been thoughtless, its tilling sometimes careless, and its harvesting almost always uncertain. Its record in trying to bring meaning to freedom for the former slaves of South Carolina had been fashioned largely by the number and nature of the men who lived and worked where the freedmen lived and worked,

15. Bentley, *Freedmen's Bureau*, pp. 201-2.
16. War Department, Special Order #102, Bureau Records, S. C., Vol. 25; General Orders and Circulars, *ibid.*, Vol. 26; Roster of Officers and Civilians, May and December, 1868, *ibid.*, Box 485; E. L. Deane to Howard, January 22, 1870, Bureau Records, Box 1098.
17. Report of the Assistant Adjutant General, October 7, 1872, *House Executive Documents*, 42 Cong., 3 Sess., no. 109 (serial 1566).

rather than by the laws of Congress or the decisions made in Bureau headquarters in Washington. What manner of men had they been?

First of all, the great majority were military officers, drawn from the regular army or from the Veterans Reserve Corps. Civilians did not comprise any appreciable part of the field force except for the two brief periods of January-March, 1866, and January-June, 1868; of these the majority, it would appear, sought employment with the agency mainly for economic rather than idealistic reasons. Some wanted positions because they were out of work and in need of money; others sought the work, they said, because they were southerners who had opposed the Confederacy and now found themselves jobless and friendless as a result of their Unionism.[18] A few, no doubt, were prompted by a sense of commitment about the purpose of war and a spirit of idealism about freedom's future. Martin R. Delany, for example, was a Negro officer who unquestionably viewed the work as an opportunity to aid in the elevation of his own race; another for whom idealism was mainly the motive was E. W. Everson, a white officer of the Veterans Reserve Corps, whose career with the Bureau was among the longest of any individual's. When asked at the time the Corps was disbanded whether he wished to remain as a civilian agent with the Bureau, Everson replied that he did wish to continue in order that he might be "an instrument of perpetuating the principles" for which he had left home in 1861; and, he went on, "I would wish it understood . . . that I desire no more pay for the service than will meet the necessities of life."[19]

Whatever their motive in entering the service, Bureau officials faced a bewildering array of duties to perform once in office. Their main responsibility, of course, lay in promoting the welfare of the freedmen through distributing rations to the needy, arranging transportation for the displaced, approving labor con-

18. Random samplings from many letters of application for a position support this conclusion. B. H. Manning to Scott, March 11, 1867, and A. G. McClure to Scott, May 9, 1867, Bureau Records, S. C., Box 478; B. G. Yocum to Scott, April 29, 1867, ibid., Box 479; C. O. Rolfe to Saxton, December 10, 1865, ibid., Box 472.

19. E. W. Everson to Scott, December 9, 1867, Bureau Records, S. C., Box 478; see also B. F. Randolph to Saxton, August 31, 1865, and B. F. Pratt to Saxton, September 20, 1865, ibid., Box 472.

tracts, visiting plantations, and looking after Negro schools. In addition they had an endless stream of complaints to be heard, investigated, and acted upon. One official estimated that during a single year he had about one thousand complaints to handle; most were trivial in nature but each required some kind of action by him personally, since he had neither staff nor troops to enforce any judgment he might make. The majority, he said, were brought by freedmen who "saw their grievances with big eyes." He then added this account of the general and varied nature of the complaints brought before him:

> They might refer to an alleged attempt at assassination or to the discrepancy of a bushel of pea vines in the division of a crop. They might be against brother freedmen, as well as against former slave owners and "Rebs". More than once have I been umpire in the case of a disputed jacknife or petticoat. Priscilly Jones informed me that her "old man was a-routin' everybody out of the house an' a-breakin' everything;" then Henry Jones bemoaned himself because his wife Priscilly was going to strange places along with Tom Lynch; then Tom Lynch wanted redress and protection because of the disquieting threat of Henry Jones. The next minute Chloe Jackson desired justice on Viney Robinson, who had slapped her face and torn her clothes. Everybody, guilty or innocent, ran with his or her griefs to the Bureau officer; and sometimes the Bureau officer, half distracted, longed to subject them all to some huge punishment. Of the complaints against whites the majority were because of the retention of wages or of alleged unfairness in the division of the crops.[20]

Another Bureau officer reported that, in addition to his normal duties, he had handled an average of 200 complaints a month; during a typical month 97 dealt with claims for money, 22 with disorderly conduct, 16 with unlawful entry, 14 with property disputes, 15 with labor questions, and 50 with various other matters such as family quarrels and disturbing the peace.[21]

Yet not even this service completed the duties of the Bureau officer. He found that a considerable amount of time and energy were further demanded by administration alone. John W. De Forest, a responsible officer of exceptional merit, wrote of the

20. De Forest, *A Union Officer*, p. 30.
21. Scott to Howard, June 20, 1866, Bureau Records, S. C., Vol. 11.

great variety of records that must be kept. He had to make entries in separate volumes for letters sent, letters received, endorsements on letters, transportation grants given, and orders received and issued; he also had to make written reports to his superiors about labor contracts, outrages by Negroes against whites and whites against Negroes, persons employed and implements hired by him for Bureau work, issues of food, clothing, and medicine, and the general state of freedmen's affairs. He was also directed on occasion to prepare special reports dealing with such matters as the number of blind and deformed persons within his three-county district, the number of indigent freedmen, and the general condition of growing crops. The single area of supplies for the destitute, in itself, constituted quite an exercise in paperwork. "To get them," De Forest wrote, "it was necessary to have duplicate requisitions, duplicate receipts, and duplicate invoices. . . . If I issued but one blanket and one skirt, I must make out three Bureau returns and four Quartermaster returns, supporting each set with duplicate invoices, duplicate receipts, and duplicate clothing-receipt rolls. . . . Even if I did not issue a solitary thing, I must still make out my seven returns. . . . On no account must I neglect to forward a letter of transmittal and copy the same in my book of Letters Sent." He added dryly: "As I scribbled over these acres of vouchers . . . I decided that the Romans conquered the world because they had no paper."[22]

A position in the Bureau, if conscientiously filled, thus carried with it a complex and demanding responsibility. Whether in fact most of the officials who served in South Carolina were conscientious in meeting this responsibility is not easy to say. Certainly, Assistant Commissioner Scott himself was. In directing the affairs of the agency he displayed efficiency, industry, and purposefulness; he supervised his subordinates closely to insure their faithful discharge of duty; and he did not hesitate to reprove them for careless or irresponsible performance. He reprimanded some, for example, for making false promises to freedmen, others for ignoring complaints of the freedmen, and still others for mixing socially with the whites on the ground that such behavior tended to undermine the Negroes' respect for the Bureau. He also displayed a remarkable attention to detail, ad-

22. De Forest, *A Union Officer*, pp. 39-41, 70-71, 87-88. See also *The Nation*, I (December 21, 1865), 779-80.

monishing one subordinate, for instance, for submitting a monthly postage bill that was too large and another for allowing the
freed workers in his district to plant watermelons between the
stalks of cotton in the fields.[23]

It ought to be observed in passing that, no matter how energetic his efforts, Scott's effective control over his personnel force
was limited by the peculiar status of military officers assigned to
service with the Bureau. They were, on the one hand, subject
to orders from the departmental military commander and, on
the other, to directives from Bureau headquarters. In the inevitable confusion that followed, the departmental commander in-
sisted upon a prior obedience of all officers to his office. Despite
an administrative change decided upon in Washington during
1866 that was supposed to give Scott greater authority over
military units in the state, he could still dispiritedly write at the
end of the year: "The department commander reserved to himself the right of ordering the movements of troops, and the establishment of post and garrisons. . . . Hence I was merely the
medium for the transmittal of orders."[24]

Whether the majority of his subordinates, military or civilian,
followed Scott's own example of efficiency in looking after Bureau
responsibilities is not clear-cut. So far as the evidence shows,
most seem to have done at least an acceptable job. Only a few
of the many who served with the agency were ever specifically
charged, even by native white critics, with incompetence in
office. When such accusations were made, and proved, Scott did
not hesitate to discharge the agents.[25] Occasionally, charges of
malfeasance appear to have been inspired solely by political
manuevering. In 1868, for example, a move was made to secure
the removal of an agent at Barnwell by a group that included
Robert Elliott, C. P. Leslie, and Niles G. Parker, all of whom were
carpetbaggers who were to gain notoriety in later political scan-

23. Scott to D. H. Chamberlain, September 25, 1867, Bureau Records,
S. C., Vol. 12; Scott to W. J. Harkisheimer, August 7, 1867, Bureau Records,
Box 518; Scott to W. A. Nerland, January 15, 1868, Bureau Records, S. C.,
Vol. 13, and Scott to J. E. Cornelius, June 6, 1866, *ibid.*, Vol. 11.

24. Annual Report of Scott, November 1, 1866, Bureau Records, Box
778. See also Ralph Ely to Scott, March 28, 1866, Bureau Records, S. C.,
Box 545; G. W. Gile to Scott, May 29, 1866, *ibid.*, Vol. 175.

25. Scott to Howard, July 18, 1867, Bureau Records, S. C., Vol. 12;
Scott to Howard, April 10, 1867, *ibid.*, Box 479; Scott to Howard, June 13,
1868, *ibid.*, Vol. 13.

dals of the state. Almost immediately a group of Negroes and of whites forwarded petitions denying the charges against the agent and warmly praising his character and ability. Moreover, an inspector sent by Scott to investigate exonerated the agent and went on to praise him for the meritorious conduct of his office.[26]

Even the best-known charge made against the Bureau in South Carolina appears of dubious warrant. Sidney Andrews, during his tour of the state in the fall of 1865, painted a highly unflattering portrait of the official at Orangeburg, a lieutenant of a New York regiment. "He doesn't really intend to outrage the rights of the negroes," Andrews wrote, "but he has very little idea that they have any rights except such as the planters choose to give them. His position . . . is a difficult one; and he brings to it a head more or less muddled with liquor, a rough and coarse manner, . . . and a hearty contempt for 'the whole d—n pack o' niggers.'" Andrews, no doubt, was honest in his comments about the personal qualities of the officer, but he was mistaken in identifying him with the Bureau, for in fact the lieutenant, William H. K. Meeker, was merely an officer with the Federal garrison stationed at Orangeburg and not a representative of the Bureau at all.[27] To be sure, he probably was looking after affairs of the freedmen of the city under orders from his commander, since military units in the South during the months following the close of the war were exepected to perform such service; but it is unfair to use Andrews' mistaken classification of the officer as a valid commentary upon the caliber of the Bureau's personnel in South Carolina.

During its own day the Bureau was frequently charged by white leaders in the state with harboring dishonest officials and condoning their misdeeds; and writers of a later generation have sometimes voiced a similar judgment about the agency. Yet such a view ignores Scott's diligence in ferreting out dishonesty, and his practice of sending inspectors from time to time to inquire into the affairs of local Bureau offices. Of more than two hundred and fifty individuals who served with the agency

26. Citizens of Barnwell to Scott, February 12, 1868; Negro group to Scott, February 15, 1868; whites to E. W. Everson, February 25, 1868; and E. W. Everson to Scott, February 28, 1868, Bureau Records, S. C., Box 481.

27. Andrews, *South Since the War*, p. 24. The Lieutenant's position is indicated in a letter by the commander of the district. E. A. Kozlay to Saxton, December 12, 1865, Bureau Records, S. C., Box 472.

in some capacity during its existence, not more than twenty or twenty-five were ever charged specifically with fraud or corruption; and in every case those against whom such charges were proved were promptly removed from office.[28] In South Carolina, at least, the Bureau seems to have been generally free of corrupt office-holders.

Though most officials were innocent of the charge of dishonesty, a number were guilty of what might be termed ethical improprieties by operating plantations as a sideline to their Bureau work. Since no order specifically forbidding the practice existed until May of 1866, and since Rufus Saxton appears to have been relatively indifferent towards the matter, several agents and officers had engaged in planting operations during 1865. Generals Joseph Fullerton and James B. Steedman, who were sent by the President on a tour of inspection of the Bureau in the spring of 1866, found that in this, as in other areas, Saxton's administration had been characterized by "mistakes and blunders" whose results had been "extremely pernicious." They strongly praised General Scott for correcting those mistakes and for his general conduct of affairs, though they did find that two local agents were still engaged in extensive planting operations.

The most notorious case involved Brigadier General Ralph Ely, whose headquarters were at Columbia. The investigators reported that Bureau business within the five-county district was being grossly neglected by Ely because of his involvement in running five rented plantations. Two, known as Hopkins Turnout, were being leased for an annual rental of $5,000, and the other three for $2.50 per acre; a sharecrop arrangement was being used under which the Negro workers were to get one-half of the proceeds from all crops grown, minus the amount advanced them in rations during the season.[29] Scott, upon learning the information, launched his own supplementary investiga-

28. This estimate is based upon a careful searching of the records and newspapers of the day for instances of dishonesty among Bureau officials. For examples of the prompt removal of dishonest agents, see James P. Low to Saxton, November 24, 1865, Bureau Records, S. C., Box 472, and E. W. Everson to Scott, January 27, 1868, *ibid.*, Vol. 44.

29. The full report of Fullerton and Steedman for South Carolina can be found in the Charleston *Courier*, June 16, 1866. Saxton's reply to their criticisms of his administration is partially given in *The Nation*, III (July 5, 1866), 3.

tion, which not only confirmed the findings of Steedman and Fullerton but also reported that Ely had issued large numbers of government rations to able-bodied workers at Hopkins Turnout. The assistant commissioner immediately dismissed Ely from service and found private individuals to assume management of the five plantations for the rest of the year. Ely's defense was that he had taken the move under a broad grant of discretion from General Saxton to provide work and a livelihood for freedmen in the Columbia region. But this commentary, though containing an element of truth, would hardly explain away the profits he realized from the crops, or his serious neglect of Bureau affairs.[30] Yet the case served its purpose. The attendant publicity, together with Scott's stern warnings to his subordinates about similar conduct and his peremptory removal of those who ignored such warnings, virtually eliminated the practice by the close of 1866.

One final consideration concerning the personnel of the Bureau in South Carolina is the matter of whether they engaged in politics within the state. Were there many, as native white spokesman so often charged, who used their office and influence to promote the cause of Radical Republicanism among the freed Negroes? To answer the question it is necessary to recall the political changes that occurred in South Carolina between 1865 and 1868.[31] Under the program of presidential reconstruction the state was seemingly started along the road towards restoration in the summer of 1865 when Benjamin F. Perry was named provisional governor and given the responsibility of supervising the process of reconstruction. Within a short time the necessary steps had been taken to repeal the ordinance of secession, revise the constitution so as to recognize the abolition of slavery, and establish a "loyal" government in the state. At an election held in November, James L. Orr, a Unionist who had opposed secession in 1860, was elevated to the governorship, members of the

30. Scott to Ely, April 4, 1866; Scott to Howard, May 13, 1866; and Scott to B. F. Faust, May 14, 1866, Bureau Records, S. C., Vol. 11; Scott to John Mansfield, June 1, 1866, ibid., Box 545; J. D. Greene to Scott, October 30, 1866, ibid., Box 488; affidavit of Ely, December 27, 1866, ibid., Box 501.

31. The account of political reconstruction which follows is based upon Simkins and Woody, South Carolina During Reconstruction, Chaps. II, III, and IV.

new legislature were chosen, and the congressional delegation selected. The restoration of South Carolina to the Union appeared complete.

But appearances proved deceptive, for when the regular session of Congress began in December, 1865, Congress made clear its determination to have a legislative voice in formulating a reconstruction program for the South. Southern states, they believed, should not be readmitted until they had demonstrated a greater willingness to measure out full justice to the emancipated slaves and a more convincing attitude of contrition about their Confederate adventure. Many congressional leaders saw in the "black codes" which Southern legislatures had drafted to regulate the affairs of Negroes an attempt to re-establish slavery in slight disguise; and they were disappointed that no state of the South had been willing to offer even a limited suffrage to qualified Negroes.

Spurred, led, and driven by Radical members, Congress began its attack on the presidential handiwork by refusing to admit to the House and Senate southern representatives who appeared to claim seats in the two bodies. Then in the middle of 1866 sufficient majorities in both houses were secured to override Johnson's veto in passing a bill to prolong the life of the Bureau for two more years. Finally, with their numbers increased by the November elections of that year, the Radicals were ready to institute their own program of reconstruction in March, 1867. As developed by the original act and supplementary bills, the congressional program began by declaring that, with the exception of Tennessee where Radical sympathizers had gained power, the state governments existing in the former Confederacy since 1865 were "provisional" only. It then grouped them into five military districts, each under the command of a major general who was charged with the responsibility of supervising the reconstruction process. In each state a constitutional convention was to be chosen by an electorate which included Negro male adults and excluded those white citizens disqualified under terms of the pending Fourteenth Amendment. The convention was to draft a new constitution which, among other things, must incorporate the same suffrage conditions; the document must then be ratified by a majority of qualified voters and approved by Congress. Finally, when the state legislature chosen under the consti-

tution had ratified the Fourteenth Amendment, and when that
Amendment had been ratified by the requisite number of states
to become operative, each of the former Confederate states could
reclaim its place in the Union.

Under this reorganization South Carolina became a part of
the Fifth Military District, whose initial commander was General
D. E. Sickles. After a few months he was succeeded by General
E. R. S. Canby, under whose direction the new program of restoration was begun. First came the registration of voters who
could qualify under the Reconstruction Acts; one hundred and
forty-eight thousand registered, of whom almost eighty-one
thousand were Negroes. Then came the election of a constitutional convention which assembled in January, 1868; of the one
hundred and twenty-four delegates, seventy-six were Negroes,
two-thirds of whom had been slaves only a few years before. The
new constitution created universal manhood suffrage, abolished
distinctions based on race or color, called for universal free education, and introduced a number of political and legal reforms.
After overwhelmingly approving it in a referendum, voters then
cast ballots for the election of members of the new state government. In that election the Republicans scored a decisive victory,
controlling the governorship, twenty-five of the thirty-one seats
in the senate, and all but fourteen of the one hundred and twenty-
four seats in the house. The governor-elect was none other than
Assistant Commissioner Robert K. Scott, who had been induced
to accept the Republican nomination for the office. Shortly after
convening, the new legislature ratified the Fourteenth Amendment, whereupon the state's congressional delegation was admitted to both houses of Congress; and on July 24, 1868, General
Canby announced that all his authority under the Reconstruction
Acts was remitted to the new civil government. With these
events South Carolina, in the eyes of Congress, was fully restored
to the Union.

Throughout these fifteen months of congressional reconstruction, the political life of the state was in constant turmoil. Native
whites, at first bewildered and then angered by the turn of events,
strove to achieve a solid front against the pattern imposed by
will of Congress. At the same time a large number of recently-
arrived whites from outside the state managed to establish their
leadership among the enfranchised freedmen; working mainly

through the Union League, a wartime agency founded to promote patriotism which had become transformed into a political instrument to promote Republicanism, they succeeded in organizing the great mass of Negro voters into a phalanx of support for the Republican party. Native white leaders, appalled by the prospects of former slaves now exercising the preponderance of power in politics, grew bitterly resentful over the political activity of these outsiders among them. Employing that derisive epithet of "carpetbaggers" to describe the Northern whites, they tended to regard all white Northerners within the state as agents for Radical Republicanism, so that much of their wrath and many of their charges were inevitably directed towards the officers and agents of the Freedmen's Bureau.

Greatest suspicion naturally centered around Robert K. Scott, since he had stepped from his post as head of the Bureau for two and a half years directly to the governor's chair. He was accused of having used his position to curry favor with the freedmen in order to gain their support for his political ambitions. His critics charged that, among other things, during 1867 and early 1868 he had been politically motivated in his use of funds authorized by Congress for the relief of destitution in those areas affected by critical crop failures that year. Scott's procedure had been to advance rations to those in need, taking as collateral for repayment of the sum involved liens upon the future crops. He had distributed supplies, so the charges ran, more to gain political power by building a following among the Negroes than to relieve suffering.[32] But a careful examination of the evidence shows that most of the crop-lien rations went to white farmers and planters rather than to freedmen. It is true that after he became governor he asked General Howard to continue him in charge of collecting the loans because, he said, "it will give me an influence in the central part of the State, where most of the issues have been made. . . ."[33] But this request came two months after he had relinquished his office as assistant commissioner, and not before.

Furthermore, it should be noted that Scott displayed no great eagerness to secure the gubernatorial position. He initially re-

32. *Ibid.*, pp. 182-84.
33. Scott to Howard, August 2, 1868, O. O. Howard Papers, Bowdoin College Library.

fused the nomination of the Republicans because, he wrote in declining, he was reluctant to transfer the heavy responsibilities of his present office to less experienced shoulders. Not until about a week later, for reasons that are unclear, did he change his mind and accept the nomination.[34]

At least until he was nominated for the governorship, Scott also worked to prevent his subordinates from engaging in politics. For example, he sternly rebuked D. H. Chamberlain—later to become governor of the state—for political activity, and he acted promptly to remove those agents who, in spite of his injunctions, gained election to political office while still serving with the Bureau.[35] When four Bureau officials were elected to membership in the constitutional convention of 1868, he immediately moved to revoke their Bureau appointments. One of the four, Gilbert Pillsbury, appealed to General Howard to be reinstated in his Bureau post as superintendent of the Shaw Orphan Asylum in Charleston, or at least to have his wife named as his successor. Howard in turn left the matter to the discretion of Scott, who refused to grant either of Pillsbury's requests. His action drew praise from one of the leading papers in the state, which commended his "judgment and sound discretion" in this matter as well as in his general conduct of the Bureau.[36] Scott himself vigorously denied a charge by the Charleston *Mercury* in December, 1867, that the Bureau was extensively engaged in politics, writing the editor that there was not "a single salaried Agent of the Bureau who is a candidate for office" or who was "a member of the Union League, or any other organization of a political character." No doubt he overstated the case in this sweeping assertion, but every sign points to an honest effort by him to make the statement become true.[37]

He also labored to impress upon the enfranchised freedmen the need to use their political power wisely. At the city of Marion, for example, he cautioned a large Negro gathering against neglecting their farm work to attend political meetings and he strongly urged them to avoid forming a party based on color

34. F. L. Cardoza and others to Scott, March 6, 1868, and Scott's reply, March 10, 1868, R. K. Scott Papers, in private possession.

35. Anderson *Intelligencer*, June 26, 1867.

36. Howard to Scott, December 11, 1867, Bureau Records, S. C., Box 479; Columbia *Daily Phoenix*, December 25, 1867.

37. Scott to Howard, December 23, 1867, Bureau Records, S. C., Vol. 12.

alone, pointing out that such a development would seriously impair race relations with the whites.[38] On another occasion he sharply rebuked a group of freedmen for having created a disturbance while registering to vote; were it not for their ignorance, he said, they would be punished severely. He closed by warning them that such behavior in the future was likely to create racial discord that would seriously injure the Negroes themselves.[39] Such firm words obviously do not suggest that Scott was using his Bureau office to build a political following among the Negroes.

By any test of resonableness, Scott was politically circumspect in his position as assistant commissioner, at least up until his nomination for the governorship, in March, 1868. However, from this time until his election and inauguration three months later, he did undoubtedly use his office and influence to advance his political ambitions. During this period he apparently expected Bureau officials to use their office to promote his election, and on at least one occasion he gave $500 to an agent to be used for campaign purposes.[40] Moreover, he was urged by supporters to distribute Bureau rations in such a way as to produce the greatest political good, though there is no evidence that he followed this advice.[41]

It is difficult to say categorically whether, throughout 1867 and 1868, the majority of officers and agents followed Scott's own example of circumspection, but it appears that most of them did. To be sure, there were several who unquestionably used their Bureau office for political ends. One was Martin R. Delany, a fiery Negro officer at Beaufort who stirred up the freedmen of his region and who ultimately was nominated for the lieutenant governorship by one wing of the Republican party. Another who very probably used his Bureau position to serve his political ambitions was Robert C. DeLarge, a mulatto from Charleston; active in politics prior to joining the Bureau in mid-1867, he was chosen a member of the constitutional convention in the latter part of that same year—a juxtaposition that suggests he utilized

38. Sumter *Watchman*, August 7, 1867.
39. Columbia *Daily Phoenix*, August 31, 1867.
40. Receipt, dated March 23, 1868, among the Scott Papers.
41. C. J. Stolbrand to Scott, March 31, 1868, Scott Papers.

his few months with the Bureau for securing political advancement.

There were at least a dozen and a half others who can be identified as men going directly from their Bureau positions to political office, or who entered politics at a later date after leaving the agency.[42] Yet even if it be assumed that all of them were politically active while serving in the Bureau—an assumption of somewhat doubtful warrant—they would still comprise but a fractional minority of the whole number of agents and officers. In sum, of a total of about one hundred and seventy-five different individuals who served with the Bureau during Scott's two-and-one-half years as its head, no more than twenty-five or thirty at the outside can be charged with politically partisan conduct.

The major historian of the Bureau has concluded that officers and agents of the agency were generally active champions of the Republican cause among the freedmen, contributing greatly towards the end "of helping the Radical politicians keep their party in power."[43] But the evidence for the state of South Carolina questions the validity of this judgment there. When the Bureau roster rolls were painstakingly compared against the most authoritative study of reconstruction in the state to determine how many of all the Republican political figures mentioned by the authors had had previous experience with the Bureau, it was found that not more than two dozen such persons, prior to entering politics, had ever been associated with the agency.[44] The great majority of individuals in the service of the Bureau, it seems clear, were basically honest men who tried to perform their duties in a responsible way. Though in the main not prompted by any deep sense of idealism in entering the service of the agency, they nevertheless worked to advance the cause of

42. Information on these individuals was gathered from a variety of sources: Simkins and Woody, *South Carolina During Reconstruction,* pp. 55, 93, 112-32; Charleston *Courier,* March 22, 1867; Charleston *Daily News,* March 9 and July 7, 1868; Rosters of Officers and Civilians for 1866-1868, Bureau Records, S. C., Boxes 484 and 485; *Harper's Weekly,* XII (November 21, 1868), 740.

43. Bentley, *Freedmen's Bureau,* p. 202.

44. Material on these persons has been secured mainly by checking the names of officeholders mentioned by Simkins and Woody, *South Carolina During Reconstruction,* Chaps., II, IV, and V, against the rosters of Bureau personnel for 1867 and 1868.

organized freedom among the former slaves of the state. That they failed to advance it more impressively was due not so much to their own human limitations as to the exceptional dimensions of the problems they faced and the inadequate means they were given in facing the challenge before them.

As the echoes of war died away in South Carolina, they left behind grim reminders that the storm of conflict had passed this way. Though the state had not been a major scene of fighting, she still had felt something of war's fury. By the spring of 1865 many of her districts lay gashed and bleeding, especially those along the coast where military operations had gone on during most of the four years of conflict. Charleston had experienced a particular anguish, strangled as she had been by the Federal blockade, pounded relentlessly by Union shelling, and gutted by disastrous fires and explosions. A Northern journalist described her as a city "of ruins, of desolation, of vacant houses, of widowed women, of rotten wharves, of deserted warehouses, of weed-wild gardens, of miles of grass-grown streets, of acres of pitiful and voiceful barrenness."[1]

Nor was Charleston alone in her devastation. Sherman's army, like a band of avenging furies, had cut a blackened swath of forty miles through the heart of the state, from border to border. The capital city of Columbia, once proud and beautiful, had been reduced to smoldering rubble, a city whose streets were now filled "with rubbish, broken furniture and groups of crouching, desponding, weeping women and children." Two-thirds of the town lay in ashes and every house except a few on the campus of the state college had been pillaged.[2] Districts in other parts of the state had also felt some of the ravages of war, either because of raids by Union cavalry or because of destruction by Confederate forces in retreat. And to the physical ruins of conflict were added the other woes of war: the human loss in killed and wounded, the suffering from critical shortages, the dislocations of people, the destruction of railroads, and the collapse of the financial structure. South Carolinians, in short, faced a bleak and barren future as they stood amidst the ashes of war.

1. Sidney Andrews, *The South Since the War* (Boston, 1866), pp. 10-11.
2. Francis B. Simkins and Robert H. Woody, *South Carolina During Reconstruction* (Chapel Hill, 1932), p. 5.

Such was the setting of desolation facing the Bureau in the summer of 1865. The need, above all else, was for deeds of charity. In a literal sense, the Bureau must feed the hungry and clothe the naked. It must seek to bind up the wounds of war and point the way towards ordered freedom for the former slaves, else its responsibility would go unfulfilled and the challenge of the times unanswered. Reports from various localities told of the urgency of the need, especially among the freedmen. One touring journalist, for example, wrote the following description of a camp of displaced Negroes in Charleston: "Families were cooking and eating their breakfasts around smoky fires. On all sides were heaps of their humble household goods—tubs, pails, pots and kettles, sacks, beds, barrels tied up in blankets, boxes, baskets, bundles. They had brought their livestock with them: hens were scratching, pigs squealing, cocks crowing, and starved puppies whining. . . ." "A more wretched and more pitiable herd of human beings I never saw," he added.[3]

After becoming assistant commissioner, Rufus Saxton moved as quickly as circumstances would permit in organizing relief for the destitute within the state, especially along the coast where the need was greatest. As authorized by law of Congress, he requisitioned surplus food from the Commissary General of the Army, clothing from the Quartermaster General, and medical supplies from the Surgeon General. He also appealed to private groups in the North to aid in gathering additional supplies. As a result of these efforts, the Bureau, by midsummer of 1865, was distributing more than three hundred thousand rations to almost nine thousand persons.[4] At the same time Saxton and his subordinates undertook to establish camps where destitute and dislocated Negroes could be fed, housed and clothed while awaiting transportation to other regions where work could be found. In addition, an asylum in Charleston was opened to care for Negro orphans.[5]

3. John T. Trowbridge, *The South: A Tour of Its Battle-Fields and Ruined Cities* (Hartford, 1866), p. 537.

4. As officially defined by the War Department, a ration consisted of prescribed ounces of beef, pork, or bacon; bread; corn meal; beans, peas, or hominy; sugar; vinegar; salt and pepper; candles and soap. In addition, limited amounts of either coffee or tea might be issued to women and children. *House Executive Document,* 39 Cong., 1 Sess., no. 11 (serial 1255), p. 47.

5. O. O. Howard, *Autobiography of Oliver Otis Howard* (New York,

Throughout the year of 1865, the agency continued its program of relief, though the scale grew smaller and not larger. By September the number of rations issued monthly had dropped to ninety-eight thousand, and by the end of December to sixty thousand.[6] The cutback reflected in part a growing measure of recovery within the state from the effects of war, and in part Saxton's wish to promote self-reliance among the freedmen. It reflected also General Howard's concern that rations be used only to prevent extreme suffering. "Assistant Commissioners," he wrote Saxton, "are held strictly responsible that there shall be no waste, and that such issues are confined to cases where humanity evidently demands them."[7] By the close of the year about seven hundred and fifty thousand rations had been issued to perhaps twenty-five thousand persons, a few of whom were white "refugees" but most of whom were freedmen.[8] Generals Fullerton and Steedman, during their tour of inspection in 1866, claimed that the distribution of rations in South Carolina had been much too liberal, but their assertion appears to have little validity.[9] The Bureau, in fact, had rendered a humanitarian service of impressive proportion, but still one that fell considerably short of the actual need.

When General Scott assumed direction of Bureau affairs early in 1866, he undertook to find ways of curtailing even futher the program of relief. By the summer he had realized enough success to draw favorable comment from Generals Steedman and Fullerton, who noted that between December, 1865, and April, 1866, the number of freedmen receiving rations each month had dropped from 8,367 to 3,777.[10] Scott was strongly supported by General Howard, who even went so far as to rule that after October 1, 1866, no rations were to be issued except to freedmen and refugees in hospitals and orphan asylums.[11] Some of the

1907), II, 226; "Rations Issued to Freedmen," Bureau Records, S. C., Vol. 36; "Report of Rations Issued, 1865," *ibid.*, Box 487.

6. "Report of Rations Issued, 1865," Bureau Records, S. C., Box 487; Saxton to Howard, October 20, 1865, *ibid.*, Vol. 9, and June 4, 1865, Bureau Records, Box 728.

7. Howard to Saxton, December 9, 1865, Bureau Records, S. C., Box 473.

8. "Report of Rations Issued, 1865," Bureau Records, S. C., Box 487.

9. Charleston *Courier*, June 16, 1866.

10. *Ibid.*

11. Charleston *Daily News*, August 29, 1866.

agents in the state also adopted a more stringent attitude in the matter. One of them, for example, when questioned about not issuing supplies to a group of impoverished Negroes in his district, replied: "Every one of these adult persons can obtain $10 to $12 per Month & rations if he or she will accept. . . . I see no reasons why the Govt. should support able bodied freed persons."[12]

But nature and circumstance refused to be governed by human planning, as the lingering dislocations of war became heightened by crop shortages in 1865 and crop failures during 1866. As destitution persisted among both races, Scott came to recognize the necessity of increasing relief assistance. He also recognized that need was color-blind and, accordingly, authorized greater help to destitute whites by instructing his agents to construe the term "refugees" as liberally as possible. In creating the Bureau Congress had used the term to mean only those Southern whites who, because of their loyalty to the Union, had been driven from their homes. But realizing that the Bureau was confronted by a condition and not a theory, Scott's humanitarian sense refused to be bound by such narrow legalism. His attitude was most fully revealed in response to a subordinate's inquiry about how to interpret the term "refugee." Noting that large numbers of impoverished whites had applied to him for help, and expressing doubt that such families could be classed as refugees, he said, because he had found that many of their providers had been killed in Confederate service, he now wished to have the matter clarified for his guidance. Scott replied that need, and not former political allegiance, should be the governing consideration in relieving distress among the whites. "Although the latter class of cases are not strictly within the meaning of the word 'Refugee,' humanity compels their admittance to its acceptance," he wrote.[13]

And yet, despite all the Bureau's efforts, destitution persisted, and even increased. Governor James L. Orr wrote in the summer of 1866 that scarcity of food prevailed in every district of the state, and that thousands, white and black, were bound to suffer

12. J. C. Beecher to Scott, February 25, 1866, Bureau Records, S. C., Box 474.

13. Endorsement of Scott on letter of L. C. Skinner, April 14, 1866, Bureau Records, S. C., Box 533.

unless the program of aid was expanded.[14] In the face of this reality, the plans of Scott and the hopes of Howard about curtailing relief proved futile. Near the close of the year Scott reported that, since January, the Bureau had issued almost eight hundred thousand rations to freedmen and one hundred and seventy thousand to whites at a total monetary cost of about $150,000.[15]

Curiously, in spite of the fact that much of the aid had gone to destitute whites, many white spokesmen remained critical of the whole Bureau relief program. They charged that it interfered with the labor system through causing the freedmen to believe that the government would support them; that it encouraged idleness among Negro workers; and that it was carelessly, even fraudulently, administered by the agents.[16] Each of these assertions, perhaps, contained some element of truth, but a larger truth, attested to by reports from throughout the state, was that the Bureau had met a genuine need in relieving want and misery among many of both races.

The new year of 1867, Scott hoped, would be the major turning point in the relief program. Well aware that there were some Negroes who preferred to rely upon Bureau subsidy instead of upon their own resources, he resolved to limit the distribution of rations to cases of actual need. Agents were instructed to provide assistance only to destitute women and children; to inform Negro workers that rations would be withheld from all those who failed to enter into labor contracts for the year; and to announce to them that the Bureau would provide transportation to other areas for those unable to find work in their own localities.[17] But nature once more frustrated Scott's resolution. Agents and officers soon began to report about the sad plight of freedmen who, because of crop shortages in 1866, had actually wound up in debt for their year's labor and who thus were without means for sustaining themselves through the coming year. One agent told of twenty-four workers whose proceeds from the cotton crop

14. Orr to Howard, July 9, 1866, Bureau Records, Box 786.
15. Annual Report of Scott, November 1, 1866, Bureau Records, S. C., Vol. 11.
16. A detailed analysis of white attitudes and criticisms is given in Chap. VIII.
17. Endorsement of Scott on letter of J. D. Greene, January 21, 1867, Bureau Records, S. C., Vol. 129.

came to $543.43. After deductions for the supplies advanced during the year by the planter, seven were entitled to shares which ranged from $4.51 to $8.15 for the year's work; the other seventeen wound up owing more than their shares provided, leaving them in debt for amounts between $1.71 and $73.62.[18] Another officer reported the case of eleven workers whose labor contract had called for them to receive one-half of the crops grown and to pay one-half of the expenses incurred. At harvest time, the seven bales of cotton they had grown entitled them to $328.97; but against this figure stood $315.03 for expenses for the year, $83.75 for time they had lost from work, and an additional amount for supplies advanced by the planter.[19] The result, of course, was that they were deeper in debt at the end of the growing season than at the beginning. In some instances Negroes who had grown desperate over their plight turned to crime for a livelihood. In others they undertook to develop a united labor front by holding mass meetings and resolving to work for nothing less than their board plus one-half of all crops grown—a demand which most white planters stoutly rejected as excessive, because in many cases they were hardly any better off than their workers as a result of having secured advances from merchants which they now found themselves unable to repay.[20]

Nor was this the whole of the matter. Early in the growing season of 1867 crops throughout the state were severely damaged by insects and adverse weather. In May Governor Orr wrote that destitution among both races was "truly appalling" and declared that only immediate and large-scale aid would prevent actual starvation.[21] The poignant appeal of one semi-illiterate was typical of many when he wrote to Scott that he had no provisions on hand for himself or his horse, without whose labor he could not even cultivate the crops he had planted: "I havent a grain to give to my horse . . . and do General for God-almyty

18. E. W. Everson to Scott, May 11, 1868, Bureau Records, S. C., Vol. 44.

19. George Pingree to Scott, August 8, 1867, Bureau Records, S. C., Vol. 177.

20. S. Place to Scott, December 20, 1866, Bureau Records, S. C., Box 545.

21. Fairfield Herald, May 1, 1867. See also B. F. Faust to Scott, May 14, 1867, Bureau Records, S. C., Box 478.

Sake Send me Some. . . ."[22] From another locality a group of citizens sent a desperate appeal to the mayor of Boston, pleading for assistance. "We are on the eve of Starvation," they declared. "We have no way in God's world to get provisions. Only through our Friends North. . . . We are oblige[d] to turn off our hands and loose [sic] our Crops unless we can get help. . . . If there is any chance in the world to get anything to eat in your city, do for Heavens Sake Send us some and save us from Perishing."[23]

Scott himself, quickly relieved of any illusions about curtailing the relief program, estimated in early spring that the number of destitute within the state was between ten and fifteen thousand, about half of whom were whites.[24] Similar reports from the other Southern states led Congress late in March to authorize General Howard to use any uncommitted Bureau funds already on hand for the relief of destitution among all classes in the South. Under such authorization, Howard set aside half a million dollars for such relief. In addition, private societies of the North increased their benevolence and citizen committees in numerous cities staged bazaars and fairs to raise money for sending supplies to the suffering in the South.[25] To meet the crisis in South Carolina Scott acted with typical vigor. He used the $110,000 assigned to him under Howard's special allocation to procure approximately 48,000 bushels of corn, 100,000 pounds of pork, and 130,000 pounds of bacon, all of which were distributed to the needy between May and September. He also distributed clothing, cash donations, and thousands of bushels of corn from philanthropic groups and individuals in the North. In addition, under the regular program of relief with supplies drawn from the Army's commissary, the Bureau distributed 683,000 rations to freedmen and almost 200,000 to refugees between November 1, 1866, and October 1, 1867, at a monetary value of $115,000.[26] All

22. U. A. Zimmerman to Scott, June 3, 1867, Bureau Records, S. C., Box 494.
23. Citizens of Darlington, June 14, 1867, Bureau Records, S. C., Box 519.
24. Scott to Howard, March 6, 1867, Bureau Records, S. C., Vol. 12.
25. George R. Bentley, A History of the Freedmen's Bureau (Philadelphia, 1955), p. 140; Edward Bright to Scott, February 28, 1867, Bureau Records, S. C., Box 477; Scott to various benevolent societies, April, 1867, ibid., Vol. 12; Columbia Daily Phoenix, September 10, 1867.
26. Annual Report of Scott, November 1, 1867, Bureau Records, S. C., Vol. 12; reports of Scott on rations issued, 1866-1867, ibid., Box 485.

told, counting both public and private contributions, something like $300,000 was spent for the relief of destitution in South Carolina during 1867, providing at least a measure of assistance to some 25,000 persons. Never before in American history had there been such an organized effort towards such a humanitarian end. It was, in short, an endeavor of warm generosity and kind human response to great human need, made without reference to sectional boundaries or political differences. Had its spirit carried over into the realm of politics between North and South during the same period, the nation itself may well have been spared some harsh moments and unhappy memories.

The actual implementation of the relief program, of course, had depended upon the agents and officers of the Bureau, most of whom publicized the availability of supplies and then waited for the needy to come to Bureau headquarters to secure them. The frequent result was that the most deserving, too ill or feeble to travel any distance, received the smallest assistance. But at least one officer, the responsible and imaginative John W. De Forest, was determined that rations should be given according to need. Having no staff to assist him in compiling a list of destitute persons for his two-county district of Greenville and Pickens, he turned for help to the local white magistrates, with whom his relations seem to have been exceptionally good. Each of them was asked to draw up with care a list of persons in actual need in his judicial beat and to forward such information to De Forest, who then compiled a master list for determining the quantity of supplies needed. From the reports which came in he found that the magistrates had listed about 1,300 freedmen and 2,500 whites as those most in need. On this basis he requested 2,580 bushels of corn for distribution during the first month; thereafter, he reported, 1,500 bushels would suffice to prevent actual starvation. Any greater quantity would tend only to promote idleness among the class "of 'low-down' whites" for whom he felt contempt, not compassion.[27] When the supplies arrived

27. In his memoir about his Bureau service De Forest reported that dialogues such as the following occurred daily between him and some "low-down white":
    "Morning. How you git'n 'long? Got anything for the poor folks?"
    "Nothing at all. Not a solitary thing."
    "Got any corn?"
    "No."

De Forest notified the magistrates who, always at the expense of their own time and often of their money as well, came to Bureau headquarters, picked up the rations for their own judicial beats, and then attended to the actual distribution. De Forest praised them highly for their selfless labor and responsible concern in seeing that relief supplies reached those who were most in need. His final report indicated that assistance had been given to 1,666 persons in the two counties of his district; of these, 813 were white and 853 were Negro.[28]

Whatever the method, whether that of De Forest or the less systematic approach of his colleagues, the Bureau provided help at the most critical moment in South Carolina since the close of the war. With the gathering of the crops in the fall, the worst was over. But it became readily apparent that the harvest was not bountiful enough to carry the people entirely through another year. Since the special Bureau funds were exhausted, and since Howard was more determined than ever to reduce the scope of the relief program, Scott asked that he be allowed during 1868 to use more extensively a crop-lien system he had earlier used with success on a small scale. Under the proposed arrangement, planters would receive Bureau rations for distribution among their Negro workers and, in return, would give the Bureau a lien against their crops as collateral for repayment of the monetary worth of the rations. In making his request, Scott noted that when he had used the scheme in a limited way during earlier years, all the loans had been faithfully repaid.[29]

Convinced by Scott's argument, Howard endorsed the plan and then advanced an initial sum of Bureau funds to launch it. But so great was the demand for crop-lien rations that Scott soon sought additional money for expanding the program. Ultimately he secured about $300,000 with which he purchased 135,000

"Got any close?"

"No."

"Ha'n't got anything'?"

"No. I told you so at first."

"Didn't know but you had somethin'. I thought I'd name it to you." John W. De Forest, *A Union Officer in the Reconstruction* (New Haven, 1948), p. 67-68.

28. *Ibid.*, pp. 75-89; De Forest to Scott, August 30, 1867, Bureau Records, S. C., Box 526.

29. Scott to Howard, January 1, 1868, Bureau Records, S. C., Vol. 13.

bushels of corn and 721,000 pounds of bacon to be used in the program.[30] As finally evolved, the arrangement called for supplies to be advanced to any planter, white or black, whom the local Bureau agent judged to be unable to maintain himself and his workers during the year. The general rule was that no more than one bushel of corn and six pounds of bacon per month were to be issued to each adult worker on a plantation. Planters were charged at the market price of $1.45 per bushel of corn and 17¢ per pound of bacon, plus an interest rate of 7 per cent. As security they had to offer a lien against their growing crops and to recognize the right of the Bureau agent to seize the crops if, in his opinion, such action became necessary to safeguard the interests of the agency.[31]

Because records are incomplete, it is difficult to know precisely how many persons, white and black, were advanced rations by the Bureau during 1868 under the crop-lien arrangement, but the number was probably between fifteen hundred and two thousand. How many workers they employed, and thus how many persons were actually fed and sustained during the year by such rations, is impossible to say. Nor is there any way of determining absolutely whether the majority of those to whom supplies went were white planters or Negroes who owned or leased their lands, though it seems probable that a majority were whites. The amounts of indebtedness incurred by various individuals ranged all the way from $8.14 on small units to more than $2,000 on large plantations.[32] In administering the program, Scott firmly admonished his subordinates to investigate each request carefully and to take all due precautions against possible fraud by applicants. On the whole they appear to have heeded his advice, at least insofar as their limited facilities would permit. Late in the summer both Howard and Scott sent separate investigators to evaluate the program, and both agreed that agents generally had been circumspect in discharging their re-

30. Annual Report of J. R. Edie, October 19, 1868, Bureau Records, S. C., Vol. 13; E. W. Everson to Scott, July 6, 1868, *ibid.*, Vol. 44.

31. Scott to Howard, March 18, 1868; Scott to George Gile, April 1 and 8, 1868; Scott to Joseph Greene, June 18, 1868, Bureau Records, S. C., Vol. 13.

32. Annual Report of J. R. Edie, October 19, 1868, Bureau Records, S. C., Vol. 13; E. W. Everson to Scott, July 6, 1868, *ibid.*, Vol. 44.

sponsibilities and insuring that supplies went only to those whose need for help was genuine.[33]

The crop-lien program unquestionably served a worthwhile need during 1868, for without it a large number of planters would have found it impossible to feed themselves and their workers during the growing season. Many people within the state thus had reason to feel gratitude towards the Bureau for its help. Yet once the crops were harvested, a great majority of those who had incurred debts for crop-lien rations showed little disposition towards repaying the Bureau, many disposing of their crops before local agents could seize them. Their unwillingness to meet their obligations came partly from inability—a Bureau inspector frankly reported that most had not made enough both to repay their loans and to sustain themselves during the year ahead—and partly from a widespread impression that they were to be given a one-year extension on their crop-lien debts.[34] Moreover, some questioned the legal validity of their obligations and, upon the advice of their lawyers, planned to challenge the matter in court.[35]

Responsibility for collecting the crop-lien debts continued to be Scott's, for even though he was governor of the state after June, 1868, he had been continued in charge of the program at his own request. In October, for reasons that are unclear but which probably grew out of his desire to strengthen his political position, he successfully appealed to Howard for authorization to postpone repayment of loans for one year in hardship cases. As a result, a board of three members was created, consisting of Assistant Commissioner John R. Edie, Colonel James P. Low, and William Aiken, a former governor of the state. The board's main purpose was that of considering all requests for suspension of payment until November, 1869.[36] Of those who owed money, only 337 even bothered to file applications for suspension; and of these, about one-third were ordered to repay their loans at once,

33. F. D. Sewall to Howard, June 18, 1868, Bureau Records, S. C., Box 481; E. W. Everson to Scott, July 6, 1868, *ibid.*, Vol. 44.

34. E. W. Everson to Scott, November 13, 1868, Bureau Records, S. C., Vol. 44.

35. C. C. Bowen to Scott, October 20, 1868, MS., S. C. Historical Society; Charleston *Daily News*, December 14, 1868.

36. Howard to Scott, October 19 and November 21, 1868, MS., Scott Papers.

while the others were given full or partial postponement of their obligations for the year.[37] But in spite of all considerations of the board and the continuing exertions of Scott, only $85,000 out of the original $300,000 advanced had been collected by the end of the year; and renewed efforts during 1869 brought in no more than $25,000.[38] In short, about $190,000 was still outstanding at the beginning of 1870; and although Scott appointed special collection agents to work on a commission basis, and instituted legal action against several defaulters, the bulk of this sum was never repaid. It was on this unhappy note that the Bureau's relief program in South Carolina was closed out.[39]

During the same years in which it was seeking to feed the hungry, the Bureau was also endeavoring to provide medical care for the sick and suffering. Under the direction of W. R. De Witt as surgeon-in-chief for the state, a medical department was organized and put into operation during the summer and fall of 1865. Several camps were created where the sick and the destitute could be temporarily cared for, and a number of hospitals and dispensaries established. So critical was the need for trained physicians that a number of native doctors, several of whom had served the Confederacy, were employed on a contract basis to attend to the medical needs of the freedmen and those whites eligible as "refugees."[40] By November the medical department consisted of sixteen physicians and twenty-nine attendants; three hospitals and twelve dispensaries, all but two of which were along the coast, had been established; and some fifteen hundred whites and seven thousand freedmen had received medical attention.[41] By De Witt's own testimony, there were, in all proba-

37. "Minutes of the Commission," Bureau Records, S. C., Vol. 34; J. R. Edie to Howard, December 31, 1868, ibid., Vol. 13, and January 29, 1869, ibid., Vol. 14.

38. J. R. Edie to Howard, January 4, 1869, and Edie to C. H. Wright, January 20, 1869, Bureau Records, S. C., Vol. 14; W. F. De Knight to various agents, September, 1869, and to Howard, January 13, 1870, ibid., Vol. 68½.

39. C. H. Wright to the Assistant Adjutant General, December 22, 1870, Bureau Records, Box 762, and March 15, 1871, Box 763.

40. W. R. De Witt to Saxton, August 14, 24, and 27, 1865, Bureau Records, S. C., Vol. 73; Charleston Courier, August 24, 1865; "Weekly Medical Report," October 7, 1865, Bureau Records, S. C., Box 497.

41. De Witt to Saxton, November 16, 1865, Bureau Records, S. C., Vol. 73; De Witt to Howard, October 21, 1865, Bureau Records, Box 728-A; Annual Report of Saxton, December 6, 1865, Bureau Records, Box 732.

bility, at least as large a number of cases left untreated for want of funds and personnel. Yet obviously, the suffering would have been even greater had there been no Bureau. And, interestingly, some of the hard-worked doctors still found occasional moments for research in behalf of science for, according to General Howard, "A number of the medical officers . . . are . . . investigating the subject [of the weight of the brain of the freedmen], and it is . . . expected that . . . many interesting statistics will be added to the archives of the bureau."[42]

In his efforts to expand the work of the medical department, the surgeon-in-chief continued to be handicapped by want of funds and by difficulty in persuading Federal military officials in the state to release medical officers from the army for service with the Bureau. Yet he persisted and by the end of 1866 could report some slight expansion of activities. Seventeen doctors were in the field, five of whom were located in towns of the interior of the state and the rest along the coast. Hospitals were in existence in five towns, occasionally receiving some financial support from local authorities in co-operation with the Bureau. Where hospitals were non-existent, physicians maintained dispensaries, normally devoting each morning to out-patients and each afternoon to visiting the critically ill in their homes. During a typical week an average of four hundred whites and two thousand freedmen were given medical care of some sort. In all, by the close of the year Bureau physicians had treated nearly five thousand whites and more than forty-one thousand freedmen.[43] For the remaining two years of its program the medical department maintained its operation at about the same level. During 1867 treatment was given to about fifty-one thousand freedmen and seven thousand whites; three hospitals with a total bed-capacity of two hundred and seventy-five had been in operation. During the following year over fifty thousand freedmen and five thousand whites were given medical attention.[44]

42. *House Executive Document*, 39 Cong., 1 Sess., no. 11 (serial 1255), p. 22.

43. W. R. De Witt to Scott, February 19, 1866, and to Charles Page, June 30, 1866, Bureau Records, S. C., Vol. 74; "Weekly Medical Reports, 1866," *ibid.*, Box 495; A. J. Wakefield to De Witt, August 28, 1866, *ibid.*, Vol. 117; A. G. Happusett to Scott, November 1, 1866, Bureau Records, Box 778.

44. Reports of M. K. Hogan, April and October, 1867, Bureau Records,

By the end of 1868, in accord with orders from Washington the surgeon-general in the state had made the necessary plans for discontinuing the work of the medical department. Hospitals were closed or turned over to local authorities for support, dispensaries discontinued, and the remaining property sold at public auction.[45] Limited though its funds and personnel had been, the medical arm of the Bureau had still managed to bring considerable relief to many of those who were suffering. Between the summer of 1865 and the close of 1868 it had treated nearly one hundred and fifty thousand cases of illness among the Negroes of the state and twenty thousand among the whites. Though the relief of suffering is hardly measurable with statistics, still the figures suggest something of the human good accomplished by the Bureau, particularly when one recalls how widespread the social distress was within the state at the close of the war. Not all the needs had been met, nor all the illness treated; but the dimensions of human suffering had been lessened—in itself a praiseworthy achievement by any institution, and especially by one whose resources were as meager as were those of the Bureau.

One final form of assistance given by the Bureau in the postwar years was that of transportation for persons displaced by war. Because means were so limited, this program never became large enough to aid more than a small number of dislocated freedmen. Nor are the records complete enough to give any very exact count of those involved, but such figures as do exist suggest that perhaps four thousand freedmen and possibly five hundred whites received free transportation from the Bureau to enable them to return to their original homes or to go to localities where they could find work.[46]

Viewed in its entirety, the relief program of the Bureau in South Carolina stands as a bright chapter in the history of the

---

S. C., Box 496; Hogan to Scott, November 1, 1867, *ibid.*, Vol. 76; "Refugees and Freedmen Treated," *ibid.*, Vol. 75; Annual Report of J. R. Edie, Ocotber 19, 1868, *ibid.*, Vol. 13.

45. Annual Report of J. R. Edie, October 19, 1868, Bureau Records, S. C., Vol. 13.

46. *The Nation*, I (December 28, 1865), 812-13; Trowbridge, *The South*, p. 537; "Transportation Granted, 1865," Bureau Records, S. C., Vol. 35; Annual Report of Scott, November 1, 1866, Bureau Records, Box 778.

institution. The figures alone are impressive. Between the summer of 1865 and the close of 1868, the Bureau had distributed almost three million rations, apart from its work of relief under the crop-lien system; given treatment to nearly 175,000 medical cases; and provided transportation for about 4,500 persons. It seems probable that during the three-and-a-half-year period, at least 125,000 different persons received assistance of some kind from the Bureau's relief efforts. Those responsible for this work of humanity could take pride in the realization that much good had been accomplished and much suffering relieved by a program of compassion and deep social concern.

Freedom in most ways was a vague and elusive thing for the ex-slaves of South Carolina, but in one respect, at least, it took on a real and concrete meaning. That was the matter of owning the land. Accustomed for generations to thinking of all that they were not, and yet longed to be, the ex-slaves seemed to see in land ownership the symbolic and actual fulfillment of freedom's promise. Their yearnings and hopes found expression in the phrase, "forty acres and a mule," which, by war's end, had become widely popular among them, both as a slogan and as an article of faith. It was not, as they expressed it, a matter either of greed or of revenge against their former masters. It was, instead, the expression of a people's aspiration to be free in a way that they could see and feel and measure, the voicing of a dream to own the land which for so long had owned them.

By the close of 1865 thousands of freedmen had become obsessed with the belief that the same government which had set them free was now going to provide forty-acre plots by distributing among them the plantations of their former owners. Almost all observers noted how they equated freedom with land ownership. A Northern journalist who had traveled extensively in the state wrote a report that was typical: "The sole ambition of the freedman at the present time appears to become the owner of a little piece of land, there to erect an humble home, and to dwell in peace and security at his own free will and pleasure: . . . in one word to be *free* to control his own time and efforts without anything that can remind him of past sufferings and bondage."[1] Negroes themselves pointedly asked the question, "What's the use to give us our freedom if we can't stay where we were raised, and own our houses where we were born, and our little pieces of ground?"[2] Native whites observed the feeling and felt disturbed about it. One of them, an editor of a rural weekly, expressed

1. *The Nation*, I (September 28, 1865), 393.
2. *Ibid.*

his concern over the persistence of the belief among the freedmen that they were to receive free farms and then complained: "But it is among the lower class . . . who think that all they have to do hereafter is to live out of somebody else's corn crib . . . that this mistaken notion has found the most numerous and sincere believers."[3]

Though the Bureau had not been the creator of this dream of the freedmen, still, if it would give greatest substance to their freedom, it must become the translator of that dream—the instrument by which their deep yearning might come to know reality. Many of the former bondsmen expectantly hoped that the Bureau would become a kind of Moses, leading them literally to the promised land. And initially there appeared to be good reason for such a hope, since at its creation the agency was given control over a sizable amount of land in the South and, seemingly, the right to sell it or to rent it in forty-acre plots to the former slaves. Most of this property had been seized during the war by Federal officials under the sanction of one or another congressional law. The first major measure of Congress looking towards the seizure of Southern property had come in 1862 with the direct tax law, according to whose terms the President was authorized to name special commissioners for those states and districts where a direct tax, levied the year before, could not peaceably be collected; such commissioners, once Federal authority had been restored, were to make assessments upon all real estate and, in cases where the owners failed to pay the tax, to declare such property forfeited to the United States. Another measure, passed by Congress later in 1862, declared all property of civil and military officers of the Confederate government subject to seizure by the Federal government, provided only that it first be condemned by court action. In the following year a third congressional measure provided for the seizure of Southern property abandoned by an owner who was "voluntarily absent" in support of the Confederacy. All the properties in the South seized under these measures and still remaining under Federal control at war's end were turned over to the Bureau during the spring and summer of 1865.[4]

3. Sumter *Watchman*, November 22, 1865.
4. The provisions of the acts and an extended discussion of each can

In South Carolina the Bureau acquired control over an additional amount of property along the coast as a result of General Sherman's action in January, 1865. Before turning northward from Savannah to the Carolinas, he wished to relieve his army of the encumbering horde of freedmen who had flocked into his lines during the preceding months. Accordingly, he directed that all the sea islands south of Charleston, and all abandoned rice fields along the rivers to a depth of thirty miles, be set apart for their use. Negro families were to be settled on forty-acre plots of such land and given what were termed "possessory titles" to them.[5]

Whatever the source, the Bureau in South Carolina during 1865 acquired control over some three hundred thousand acres of land and about one thousand pieces of town property. Immediately upon assuming office as assistant commissioner, Saxton made clear his determination to use the land to provide refugees and freedmen with forty-acre homesteads, "where by faithful industry they can readily achieve an independence."[6] He and other assistant commissioners were reassured of the correctness of such a policy by General Howard, who in midsummer issued Circular No. 13, outlining a systematic procedure to be followed in the matter. Assistant commissioners were instructed to set apart all lands coming under their control and to begin selling them or renting them in forty-acre plots. Such plots were to be leased for three-year periods for annual rentals not to exceed six per cent of the appraised value in 1860; at any time within the lease period the occupant was to enjoy the right to purchase the land, receiving "such title as the United States can convey." On the question of whether President Johnson's Amnesty Proclamation, issued earlier, applied to Bureau-held lands, Howard's circular was quite explicit: "The pardon of the President will not be understood to extend to the surrender of aban-

be found in J. G. Randall, *Constitutional Problems Under Lincoln*, rev. ed. (Urbana, 1951), pp. 275-80, 316-41.

5. *War of the Rebellion: A Compilation of the Official Records of the Union and Confederate Armies* (Washington, 1880-1901), ser. 1, XLVII, part 2, 60-62. For a full account of the whole matter, see Willie Lee Rose, *Rehearsal for Reconstruction: The Port Royal Experiment* (Indianapolis, 1964), Chap. XII.

6. Circular #1, June 10, 1865, Bureau Records, S. C., Box 496.

doned or confiscated property which by law has been 'set apart for refugees and freedmen.' "[7]

With energy and determination, Saxton proceeded to execute the Bureau's program of land distribution. His philosophy in the matter was set forth by him in a long letter to Howard about the protests of the whites whose lands had been seized under law of Congress. Noting that they had "unhesitatingly cast their fortunes with the rebellion," they should now, he went on, "abide the results of their choice." As for the freedmen now occupying the lands, they deserved every assistance from the Federal government for, unlike the whites, "They have always been loyal to the Union cause, have piloted our ships through these shallow waters, have labored on our forts . . . and have enlisted as Soldiers in our Country's darkest hours to help fight in her struggle for existence." "On this soil," he added, "have they and their ancestors passed two hundred years of unrequited toil." And he then asked rhetorically, "Could a just Government drive out these loyal men who have been firm and loyal in her cause in all her darkest days . . . and are only now here because by hard fighting her cause has triumphed?"[8]

But the plans of Howard and the hopes of Saxton were soon frustrated by President Johnson. Opposed in principle to any kind of sweeping confiscation of Southern property, he had clearly stipulated in his Amnesty Proclamation of May, 1865, that presidential pardon of Southerners carried with it restoration of all rights of property except slaves. When he learned of Howard's Circular No. 13, which had been issued by the Commissioner without presidential approval, he took steps immediately to reverse the Bureau policy. Early in September he ordered Federal commanders in the South to take steps to prevent assistant commissioners from making any further seizures of abandoned lands, pending a final presidential decision about the question.[9] Then, under his personal supervision, he had prepared at the White House a new statement of policy which Howard was directed to issue as a circular superseding his earlier Circular No. 13. Dated September 12, the new directive instructed assistant commis-

7. Circular #13, July 28, 1865, Bureau Records, S. C., Box 496.
8. Saxton to Howard, August 22, 1865, Bureau Records, S. C., Vol. 9.
9. General George Meade to Saxton, September 3, 1865, Bureau Records, S. C., Box 472.

sioners to restore to pardoned Confederates all abandoned and confiscated lands except those already condemned and sold by court decree (those condemned but not yet sold were also to be returned). Freedmen living on such lands were to be allowed to retain their occupancy until they could harvest the crops they had planted. Howard sought to persuade the President to require the white owner to whom lands were returned to furnish each family of Negro occupants a small homestead, but without success; Johnson's view was that restoration rights under presidential pardon were absolute.[10]

As he witnessed these developments and saw clearly their threat to the plans of the Bureau and the dreams of the freedman, Saxton was at first incredulous and then dismayed. "It is well to forgive our enemies," he wrote in one letter to Howard, "but it is not well to be unjust to those who are loyal and faithful to their duty."[11] In another he pointed out that freedmen had been solemnly promised the Bureau-held lands and that thousands of them were already settled on forty-acre plots; he then concluded: "I trust that the government will never break its faith with a single one of these colonists by driving him from the home which he has been promised."[12] Howard himself was as deeply troubled as Saxton about Johnson's decision; in his autobiography he would recall, with a trace of biting sarcasm, that the President had persisted in his program of reconstruction, "regardless of such minor justice as making good to thousands of freedmen that promise of land which was at the time so essential to their maintenance and their independence."[13]

But neither the Commissioner nor his assistant commissioner in South Carolina felt disposed to defy the President in the matter. Accordingly, Saxton—though reluctantly and with heavy heart—began the restoration of abandoned and confiscated lands to their original owners. He also instructed his subordinates to inform the freedmen that the Bureau had no lands to assign to them, and particularly to do everything possible to correct their notions—which apparently had become widespread—that some

10. The whole story is related in George R. Bentley, *A History of the Freedmen's Bureau* (Philadelphia, 1955), pp. 92-100.

11. Saxton to Howard, September 8, 1865, Bureau Records, Box 728-A.

12. Saxton to Howard, September 9, 1865, Bureau Records, Box 728-A.

13. O. O. Howard, *Autobiography of Oliver Otis Howard* (New York, 1907), II, 241.

kind of general distribution of land was to take place at the beginning of the new year. By the end of 1865 he reported, without citing specific figures, that much of the property held as confiscated or abandoned had been returned to the white owners.[14] Saxton's successor as assistant commissioner continued the policy of restoration until by the close of 1868 only seventy-five thousand acres of the three hundred and twelve thousand originally held by the Bureau remained unrestored—and this residue was simply dropped from Bureau rolls when the agency closed out its existence in the state at the end of the year.[15]

The regular policy of restoration did not include the sea island region, however, since the lands there had been set apart for the freedmen by General Sherman's order and thus occupied a special status. Recognizing this, the President instructed General Howard personally to proceed to South Carolina to inquire into the matter and to search for an equitable solution to it.[16] Accordingly, Howard visited the sea island district on October, 1865, talked with spokesmen of the dispossessed owners, and then summoned a gathering of representatives of the freedmen to address them. An observer who was present recorded the scene:

> The church was crowded. General Howard, in simple words, said that he, being their friend, had been sent by the President to tell them that the owners of the land, their old masters, had been pardoned, and their plantations were to be given back to them; that they wanted to come back to cultivate the land, and would hire the blacks to work for them.
>
> At first the people could not understand, but as the meaning struck them, that they must give up their little homes and gardens, and work again for others, there was a general murmur of dissatisfaction. General Howard's task grew more painful. He begged them to lay aside their

14. Circular #5, October 19, 1865, as printed in the Charleston *Courier,* November 22, 1865; Annual Report of Saxton, December 6, 1865, Bureau Records, Box 728-A.

15. Annual Report of Scott, November 1, 1866, Bureau Records, Box 778; Annual Report of Scott, November 1, 1867, Bureau Records, S. C., Vol. 12; *House Executive Document,* 40 Cong., 3 Sess., no. 1 (serial 1367), pp. 1016-17.

16. Bentley, *Freedmen's Bureau,* pp. 98-99.

bitter feelings, and to become reconciled to their old masters. We heard murmurs of "No, never." "Can't do it."[17]

Finding himself pressed between the demands of the planters for restoration and the firm objections of the freedmen, Howard at length decided to turn the tangled question over to a special board of three members. Two of the three were to be representatives selected each by the Negroes and the planters, and the third was to be an officer, Captain A. P. Ketchum, to represent the Bureau. Under the direction of the board the lands were to be restored to their original owners, but on two conditions: that the freedmen occupying the lands be allowed to harvest their growing crops, and that they be offered either a reasonable labor contract or the opportunity to lease the land for the coming year.[18]

Howard then departed for an inspection of the Bureau in other parts of the South, assuming that the problem had been set on its way toward an ultimate solution. But new difficulties soon developed. Shortly after he left the planters protested over the efforts of the freedmen to elect one of their own race to the board, objecting that a Negro was not a "citizen" and hence could not be qualified to serve. Howard at length yielded to the argument and agreed to permit two white representatives, along with the Bureau officer, to comprise the board.[19] Meanwhile, Secreatry of War Stanton—who was opposed to the President's program towards the South—had received Howard's report of his action in the sea island matter and was displeased to find that he had commited the Bureau essentially to a policy of restoration. In a telegram to Howard the secretary made clear his belief that lands were to be restored *only* if an arrangement mutually satisfactory to the freedmen and the whites could be worked out. He added: "I do not understand that your orders require you to disturb the freedmen in their possession at present, but only ascertain whether a just, mutual agreement can be made."[20]

Howard's own misgivings about the rightness of President Johnson's policy needed no further reinforcing. He immediately

17. Mary Ames, *From a New England Woman's Diary in Dixie in 1865* (Springfield, 1906), pp. 96-97.

18. Bentley, *Freedmen's Bureau*, p. 98.

19. Henry E. Tremain, *Two Days of War: A Gettysburg Narrative and Other Excursions* (New York, 1905), pp. 247-51.

20. *House Executive Document*, 39 Cong., 1 Sess., no. 11 (serial 1255), p. 9.

sent orders to Captain Ketchum not to restore any of the sea island estates unless the freedmen in possession had accepted labor contracts.[21] And a short while later he instructed Assistant Commissioner Saxton not to hasten the return of any property in South Carolina.[22] Saxton hardly needed such admonition, for he had steadfastly opposed the program of restoration. On each application for restoration of a sea-island estate he had written: "The freedmen were promised the protection of the Government in their possession. This order [of General Sherman's] was issued under a great military necessity. . . . More than forty thousand destitute freedmen have been provided with homes, under its promises. I cannot break faith with them now by recommending the restoration of any of these lands."[23] A little later, in his final report as assistant commissioner, Saxton warmly recommended a plan for settling the matter on terms that would be equitable to both parties. "I would respectfully suggest," he wrote, "that a practical solution of the whole question . . . may be had by the appropriation of money by Congress to purchase the whole tract set apart by this order, . . . and offer to pay to the former owner that sum, or give him possession of the land, as he may elect. In case he should prefer the land to the money, then pay the money over to the freedman, who occupies it."[24] But the suggestion was given no serious consideration by Congress.

Complicating the matter still further was the attitude of the freedmen. Most of them obstinately refused to accept labor contracts for 1866 and angrily rejected all proposals for the surrender of their possessory titles. A Northern journalist who had accompanied a group of planters as they sought to negotiate a settlement with the freedmen on their lands told of talking with a Negro and pointing out to him that the possessory titles were possibly invalid. In reply the freedman no doubt spoke for many when he said: "If a man got to go crost de riber, and he can't git a boat, he take a log. If I can't own de land, I'll hire or lease

21. Bentley, *Freedmen's Bureau*, p. 99
22. Howard to Saxton, December 23, 1865, Bureau Records, S. C., Box 473.
23. Endorsement of Saxton, September 6, 1865, on petition of Constantine Bailey, Bureau Records, S. C., Box 487; *The Nation*, I (October 26, 1865), 515.
24. Annual Report of Saxton, December 6, 1865, Bureau Records, Box 728-A.

land, but I won't contract."[25] In some instances freedmen armed themselves and threatened violence against whites whom they suspected of coming to take the lands from them, on one occasion seizing and menacing a group of planters for five hours until Federal troops arrived to effect a rescue.[26] So intent were they upon land-ownership that once when a Negro officer of the Bureau informed them that the land must be restored to the whites, their bitter reply was that Christ had been betrayed by one of his own color.[27]

Finally, the conduct of Captain Ketchum added one more element of confusion to an already confused situation. Planters were soon protesting that, in his capacity as chairman of the board of settlement created by Howard, he was obstructing rather than faciliating the return of the lands to them. Ketchum himself, showing clearly his understanding of the will of Howard and Saxton that restoration not be hurried, revealed his view in the endorsement with which he forwarded applications for restoration of the plantations. Noting that the sea islands had been set apart for the freedmen by Sherman's order and that the Negroes had occupied the lands since early 1865, he concluded: "It is considered that these people . . . have acquired a possessory title . . . and that unless they will voluntarily give up their possessory rights this plantation can not be restored."[28] Thus the old year ended and the new began on a note of bewildering uncertainty about the future of the sea island lands.

Events of 1866 at last would pull order out of the chaos and provide a solution to the vexatious question. For one thing Captain Ketchum—probably at the insistence of President Johnson—was relieved from his post and transferred.[29] For another a delegation of prominent white leaders met with General Sherman and elicited from him the statement that he had intended his order to be only a temporary expedient and not a permanent arrange-

25. John T. Trowbridge, *The South: A Tour of Its Battle-Fields and Ruined Cities* (Hartford, 1866), pp. 539-40.

26. Charleston *Courier*, February 1, 1866.

27. B. J. Whaley to E. M. Whaley, January 11, 1866, MS., E. Mikell Whaley Papers, S. C. Historical Society.

28. Endorsement of Ketchum, February 7, 1866, on a letter from W. H. Trescot, Bureau Records, S. C., Vol. 40.

29. Special Order #27, February 24, 1866, Bureau Records, S. C., Box 476.

ment.[30] Finally, Federal military authorities in the state—again probably because of a presidential directive—intervened directly and forcefully in the matter. On January 1, 1866, General D. E. Sickles, commander of the Department of South Carolina, issued an order to his subordinates to insist that freedmen on the sea island lands enter into reasonable contracts within ten days or suffer eviction.[31] Under this order officers were dispatched to examine possessory titles held by the Negroes, judge their validity, and compel the owners of invalid ones to accept labor contracts or leave the plantation. Scott protested this action to Sickles and even went so far as to direct a Bureau officer to reinstate every titleholder expelled by the military authorities—an action which drew from Sickles the suggestion that Scott should not "countermand military orders."[32]

Confronted by the stern resolution of the military authorities, Scott at length proposed a sensible set of rules to be applied in providing an equitable solution for the complex question. With the concurrence of Sickles, these rules at last brought an end to the tangled, unhappy story. Under their provisions all owners of land within the area affected by General Sherman's order who had secured a presidential pardon could return at once and reclaim their estates (unless such lands had already been sold under court order). But two or three conditions were attached. Freedmen holding valid possessory titles were not to be disturbed, though the original owner might, with the Bureau's agreement, consolidate scattered claims on his plantation into one compact segment; those Negroes holding no possessory claims, or invalid ones, were to be compelled to leave only if they refused to accept reasonable labor contracts. Two basic considerations were to be applied in determining the validity of possessory titles held by the freedmen: the possessor of the claim must have occupied and cultivated the land in person prior to October 17, 1865, the date of General Howard's visit to the region;

30. W. H. Trescot to President Johnson, January 31, 1866, Bureau Records, Box 786.

31. General Order #1, January 1, 1866, Andrew Johnson Papers, Library of Congress.

32. The entire affair is related in the following Bureau records for S. C. for 1866: Scott to J. C. Beecher, February 26, Vol. 11; Scott to Sickles, March 16, Box 475; J. E. Cornelius to Scott, April 27, Box 475; Scott to Howard, March 27 and May 21, Vol. 11.

and he must have selected the plot from the plantation specified in the possessory title, rather than—as often had happened—holding title to one plot and settling upon another. Under these regulations, as enforced by military authority, restoration of the disputed lands proceeded steadily throughout 1866; confronted with such a reality, the bulk of the Negroes—again demonstrating that great sense of adaptability which had enabled them to endure two hundred years of bondage and still believe in better things —compromised with the inevitable and made the best of a bitter disappointment.[33]

Because the records are confusing and incomplete, it is impossible to determine the exact number of Negroes, out of the original forty thousand settled under Sherman's order, who had actually received written possessory titles to forty acres, but it seems likely that the figure was not greater than five thousand. And of this number, many held titles which, under Scott's program of restoration, were found to be invalid. Some had occupied plots either less or more than forty acres, ranging in size from four to four hundred acres; others had secured a title to land on one plantation but had settled on another; and still others had staked out their claim on one of the sea islands different from that specified in their grants. Thus, a large number of the freedmen lost their claims through error of one kind or another. Scott reported at the close of 1866 that only 1,565 had been found to be holding valid possessory titles.[34]

The story reached its ultimate conclusion in the following year when, under law of Congress, the holders of valid possessory titles were allowed to exchange them for certificates to other land around Beaufort, Hilton Head, and Port Royal to which the United States had acquired definite title. Most of them took advantage of the offer and so at long, weary last realized their hope of owning the land.[35]

But the dream of "forty acres and a mule" was more mocked than fulfilled for the thousands who had longed and hoped to

33. General Order #9, March 7, 1866, Bureau Records, S. C., Vol. 26; Scott to J. E. Cornelius, March 17, 1866, *ibid.*, Box 535.
34. Scott to Howard, March 16, 1866, Bureau Records, S. C., Vol. 11; Annual Report of Scott, November 1, 1866, Bureau Records, Box 778; Newberry *Herald,* June 4, 1866; J. E. Cornelius to Scott, October 23, 1866, Bureau Records, S. C., Box 488.
35. Circular #2, January 9, 1867, Bureau Records, S. C., Vol. 26.

own the land. For every one Negro who, with the Bureau's help, became a landowner, at least fifty others had seen the dream crumble and the hope fade. Yet the yearning, and the believing, persisted. Thousands of freedmen throughout the state continued to cling to the belief that they would get free farms in a general land distribution at the beginning of 1868. In part the lingering hope was tied up with the meeting of the state constitutional convention, which had recently assembled in accord with the congressional reconstruction program and which, many believed, would somehow provide free land. So widespread was the notion, and so deeply was it held, that in numerous districts freedmen stubbornly refused to enter into labor contracts for the new year, leading Scott to request the convention to take steps to dispel the mistaken idea. The convention responded by announcing that it had no means for securing land for distribution and then by adopting a resolution calling upon Congress to appropriate one million dollars for the purchase and resale of lands to the freedmen.[36] Such measures seemingly had their effect in settling the minds of the freedmen, since by the spring of 1868 most were reported to have accepted terms of employment for the year from the white owners. And slowly the realization spread among them that the land was not to be theirs.

A few of the bolder among them, having earlier recognized the truth that South Carolina held no hope for their dreams, had sought to realize them elsewhere by taking advantage of the Southern Homestead Act of 1866. This congressional measure had provided that lands owned by the United States in Alabama, Arkansas, Florida, Louisiana, and Mississippi were to be opened for settlement in eighty-acre plots by freedmen and refugees. During 1867, under the encouragement of the Bureau, an indeterminate number—though probably between five and ten thousand—had left the state to acquire a homestead in one of the specified states.[37] But they, like the kinsmen and friends who had stayed behind, were doomed to ultimate disappointment. The homestead program turned out to be a resounding failure, partly because the lands set aside under it were of the poorest quality,

36. Orangeburg *News*, February 1, 1868; Scott to N. G. Parker, February 10, 1868, Bureau Records, S. C., Vol. 13; *House Miscellaneous Document*, 40 Cong., 2 Sess., no. 81 (serial 1349), pp. 1-2.

37. Bentley, *Freedmen's Bureau*, pp. 144-46; Charleston *Courier*, January 21, 22, 28, 1867; New Orleans *Tribune*, October 3, 1866.

and partly because the freedmen lacked the necessary means to support themselves while working to clear the land and cultivate a crop.[38] Consequently, most wound up as laborers for some white employer. And so they, like the bulk of freedmen in South Carolina, found themselves for decades yet to come destined to remain hewers of wood and drawers of water.

Stumbling and groping their way forward from slavery towards freedom, the Negroes of South Carolina had dreamed fervently of owning the land, had, indeed, seen in its ownership the fulfillment of freedom's promise. And for many the dream momentarily became reality as they found themselves the possessor of forty-acre plots; they came so close, only in the end to find the dream crumbling and slipping between their fingers. Hopes had been raised and spirits lifted, only at last to find futility rather than fulfillment. Instinctively a large gathering of freedmen on the sea islands, when they learned that the lands were not to be theirs, expressed the anguish of a people's soul when they began to chant the old spiritual, "Nobody knows the trouble I feel—Nobody knows but Jesus."[39]

Nor was the matter wholly one of shattered dreams and broken hopes. It also had a practical consequence of major proportions. With ownership of the land to provide an underpinning, the former slaves would at least have had some prospect for making their freedom into a thing of real and meaningful substance; without it, they were bound to remain no more than half-free, victimized by an economic system that left them caught in a web of futility and despair. For nearly a century thousands in South Carolina would find, not the liberty so movingly foretold by Julia Ward Howe in her "Battle Hymn of the Republic," but a life of sharecropping, of tenancy, of poverty, of malnutrition, and of ignorance.

Sweeping confiscation of Southern lands would not have been the answer; not only would such a step have raised serious constitutional questions but, in addition, would have embittered dispossessed whites so deeply that race relations, already troubled, would probably have grown rancorous. And even if the

38. Robert H. Woody "The Labor and Immigration Problem of South Carolina During Reconstruction," *Mississippi Valley Historical Review*, XVIII (1931), 195-212.

39. Howard, *Autobiography*, II, 238-41.

Bureau had been allowed to distribute to the freedmen all of the land it held in 1865, as General Howard pointed out, it would have been able to provide no more than an acre to each Negro family. The only meaningful solution would have been for Congress to appropriate enough money to aid the Negroes in purchasing or renting land—a step which, like emancipation itself, would have required both vision and courage. But the President lacked the concern, the Congress lacked the courage, and the nation lacked the commitment. Though the freedman acquired the ballot during these years as an instrument to advance his freedom, without the land and what it represented towards economic independence, his freedom would quickly prove a fragile thing. As W. E. B. Du Bois observed more than half a century ago, to give the Negro only the ballot without the land as an economic underpinning was to end "a civil war by beginning a race feud."[40] As a consequence, the actuality of his emancipation would fall far short of its promise.

40. W. E. B. Du Bois, *The Souls of Black Folk: Essays and Sketches* (Chicago, 1918), p. 38.

Except for relief to the destitute, the most pressing problem before the Bureau in 1865 lay in organizing a system of contract labor for Negro workers, a question whose importance was heightened by the failure of the freedmen to gain ownership of the land. Though unshackled, the former slaves were still far from free, and here they would remain unless as free laborers they could gain enough security to clothe their freedom with meaning. As a race just emerging from bondage, most of them had but one commodity to sell in the economic market place, and that was the labor of their hands. The question was whether they could sell it for a return great enough to enable them to rise above the level of subsistence and realistically to dream of a brighter future. The challenge before the Bureau was that of developing a sytem in which the Negro, as a free laborer, might find hope and not despair. Nor was this all. The agency also faced the task of trying to change human attitudes. The freedmen, thousands of whom in the summer of 1865 were mistaking liberty for license as they wandered about from place to place, must be taught that as free workers they had duties as well as privileges; the whites must somehow be impressed with the necessity of recognizing and accepting the Negro's new right to bargain for his terms and conditions of employment.

Lending urgency to these considerations was the agricultural distress produced by the war and its aftermath. Since the majority of both races depended upon the soil for their livelihood, both stood to suffer severely unless stability were soon restored to agriculture, especially in the critical area of labor supply. By no means were all the freedmen seized with a wanderlust at the close of the war; some, such as those on the plantation of Governor F. W. Pickens, had taken the initiative in developing a farming system in which, according to Pickens himself, the land was never "in better condition, nor industry, good order and satisfaction more prevalent."[1] Yet sizable numbers of others had been cut adrift, emotionally and socially, and stood in need of disciplined direction for their own ultimate welfare. In short, the whole question of restoring health to agriculture was critical; the need was so great and so pressing that delay might well invite disaster. How promptly, and how well, the Bureau met the challenge would directly affect the lives of thousands of both races.

Since Federal military forces had occupied much of the coastal region as early as 1862 and had already evolved a program of free labor there, the need for Bureau action was more imperative in the interior of the state, where the dislocations of war lingered on late into 1865.[2] Indeed, so pressing was the problem that even before General Saxton could organize the forces of the Bureau, Federal military commanders were already undertaking to bring some order out of the agricultural chaos. Under a proclamation from military headquarters directing Negroes and whites to enter into equitable labor agreements, local commanders in the spring of 1865 initiated the development of a labor contract system.[3]

Typical was the work of General A. S. Hartwell, whose headquarters were at Orangeburg. Besides publishing announcements in local papers informing whites and Negroes of the necessity of entering into labor contracts, he also sent subordinates to farms and plantations throughout his two-county district to advise both groups. Within two weeks he estimated that two thousand whites and ten thousand freedmen had been contacted. In general they were told by the officers, in a common-sense manner, of the need to recognize the changed realities of a free-labor system. Whites were firmly warned that they must treat their workers as free men, while the Negroes were no less firmly told that they must live up to the terms of the contracts they accepted.

The officers wrote that they received almost uniform courtesy from the whites, most of whom seemed to be sincerely willing to accept the new order. They also reported that the freedmen

1. Edgefield *Advertiser*, June 14, 1865.
2. See Francis B. Simkins and Robert H. Woody, *South Carolina During Reconstruction* (Chapel Hill, 1932), pp. 3-20, for a description of the aftermath of war.
3. Charleston *Courier*, June 7, 1865.

listened respectfully to their remarks about the rights of freedom but often remained indifferent towards admonitions about its duties. They went on to observe that many Negroes were rejecting labor agreement because of their conviction that the lands of their former masters were to be distributed among them. And, according to one officer, among some who did enter into labor agreements, "the most reasonable fancy which prevails is that besides receiving their food, clothes, and the free rent of houses . . . they are to take for themselves all day Saturday and Sunday and to receive half of the crops."[4]

By addressing themselves to such attitudes as well as to material conditions, Federal forces in scattered parts of the interior sought to bring some order out of the social and agricultural confusion. Thus, when the Bureau began actively to function in the state in midsummer, it found the beginnings of a contract labor system established. Its main task, then, was to expand the system as rapidly as possible during the remainder of the year. Shortly after assuming office General Saxton addressed a circular to whites who still had not made contracts with their Negro workers, warning that unless they did so at once, they would be treated as disloyal citizens whose property would be subject "to seizure and divison among the freedmen."[5] But in light of the Bureau's limited personnel for enforcing such a threat, it seems unlikely that it had much effect upon the whites.

In trying to organize a systematic program of free labor, Saxton drew up for the guidance of his subordinates a model contract under whose terms Negro workers would be entitled to living quarters, rations, medical care, fuel, and a share of the crops produced, preferably one-half. He also instructed each officer to create a board of himself and two whites to superintend the contract system in the local area, the citizen members to be reimbursed for their efforts through levying upon each planter a fee of ten cents for each contract approved by the board. Bureau officials were instructed to use local courts for enforcing the terms of labor agreements, provided the civil magistrates dis-

4. C. C. Soule to O. O. Howard, June 12, 1865, Bureau Records, S. C., Box 519, and Soule to Howard, September 18, 1865, Bureau Records, Box 728. See also the Charleston *Courier*, June 26, 1865; Newberry *Herald*, July 15 and 19, 1865; and the Camden *Journal*, July 28, 1865.
5. General Order #2, June 26, 1865, Bureau Records, S. C., Box 496.

played a judicial willingness to accept Negro testimony without prejudice; otherwise, they were personally to adjudicate any labor disputes and to call upon local military commanders for any troops needed in enforcing their decisions.[6]

Within these broad outlines Bureau officials proceeded during the remainder of 1865 to extend the labor contract program. Since the records are incomplete, it is impossible to determine how many agreements were actually drawn under Bureau supervision, though a reasonable estimate would be about two or three thousand, covering perhaps thirty to forty per cent of the free workers of the state. Most of the agreements called for the Negro to receive rations and a share of the crops grown, usually from one-tenth to one-third. Some of the contracts, surprisingly, were approved with restrictive provisions strongly reminiscent of slavery; among them were terms prohibiting the workers from leaving the plantation without permission, keeping firearms or "other offensive weapons," and drinking whiskey or engaging in "other gross vices."[7] Many of the freedmen working under such terms must have wondered whether any real difference separated the new freedom from the old slavery.

Laboring as best it could under the circumstances, the Bureau strove to bring about the return of stability to agricultural life. But by harvest time it became clear that the planting year had been far from successful. From various districts came reports that told of crop shortages and grim prospects for the winter ahead. In surveying the scene in the state at the close of 1865, Saxton wrote privately that the material circumstances of the Negroes appeared actually worse than they had been under slavery.[8]

In part the farming failure of 1865 was attributable to the lingering dislocations of war and in part to the lateness of the

6. General Order #11, August 28, 1865, Bureau Records, S. C., Box 496; Saxton to E. A. Kozlay, October 20, 1865, *ibid.*, Box 533; Howard to Saxton, June 29, 1865, *ibid.*, Box 473.

7. Arney Childs (ed.), *The Private Journal of Henry William Ravenel, 1859-1887* (Columbia, 1947), pp. 239-40; G. H. Nye to Saxton, August 22, 1865, Bureau Records, S. C., Box 487; J. P. Gobin to Saxton, August 17, 1865, *ibid.*, Box 489; Ralph Ely to Saxton, November 22, 1865, *ibid.*, Box 545; contract of I. W. King and freedmen, Darlington, *ibid.*, Box 520.

8. Saxton to J. M. Hawks, November 7, 1865, MS., J. Milton and Ester Hawks Letters, Library of Congress; Charleston *Courier*, September 23, 1865.

spring planting. But a larger reason, according to most contemporary observers, had been the disorganized conditions of Negro labor, along with the unwillingness of many freedmen to work faithfully and industriously. Typical was the comment of a Northern planter of considerable experience with Negro labor when he wrote that, although he could not complain of any "extraordinary delinquencies" on the part of his laborers, he was often vexed by their "slow, shiftless habits." He was convinced, he added, "that if Northerners emigrate to the South and undertake agriculture or anything else here, they will be compelled to import white laborers."[9] In another instance, according to a foreign traveler in the state, only four hundred bales of cotton would be grown in one sea island parish which before 1860 normally produced six thousand bales; the main explanation for the decline, according to Northern planters there, had been the unreliability of the Negro workers.[10] Even General Scott, commenting on the farming failure in the coastal regions, observed that "The colored people there, finding themselves suddenly free, and with no power to guide and direct them properly, supposed that with Freedom all other things would be added. . . ."[11]

It was hardly to be expected, of course, that the freedmen, released from the compulsion of slavery and emotionally reoriented by emancipation, should suddenly have become models of industry and diligence. Nevertheless, the fact of their different work habits, along with the other factors noted, meant that the old farming year closed and the new one opened on an unpromising note. Many of the freedmen, because they had realized next to nothing for their year's labor and also because a large number persisted in their belief that they were to be given forty-acre farms, refused to enter into labor contracts at the beginning of 1866. A Bureau official in Columbia, for example, wrote that whenever the Negro workers in his district were approached about signing labor contracts, they almost invariably replied,

9. R. Soule to C. P. W., October 9, 1865, in Elizabeth W. Pearson (ed.), *Letters from Port Royal* (Boston, 1906), pp. 315-16. See also E. A. Kozlay to Saxton, August 31, 1865, Bureau Records, S. C., Vol. 250; G. H. Nye to Saxton, November 1, 1865, *ibid.*, Box 472; and Scott to Howard, May 13, 1866, *ibid.*, Vol. 11.

10. J. H. Kennaway, *On Sherman's Track* (London, 1867), pp. 53-56.

11. Scott to Howard, May 13, 1866, Bureau Records, S. C., Vol. 11.

"We will wait awhile; something will turn up."[12] Another, in the Charleston area, described the freedmen there as being "emphatically and painfully in a state of unrest." Some of them, he added, were willing to work by the job or by the day, but very few would accept contracts for the planting season ahead.[13] Moreover, a good many from the interior continued to find an attraction about the coastal region and so were gravitating there without fixed purpose or clear aims.[14]

In his closing months in office General Saxton—now laboring under the double handicap of reduced personnel and a small income for the Bureau—strove as best he could to promote a restoration of stability in agricultural life. He directed his subordinates to give unsparing attention to the making of labor agreements and again he prepared a model contract for their guidance. In form it was similar to the one he had drafted at the beginning of the Bureau's operation, with one difference. Henceforth, instead of being charged ten cents for each contract approved, planters were to be charged from twenty-five to fifty cents per worker employed—a provision which only heightened the whites' dislike of the agency.[15]

For their part, white landowners were as unhappy with the outcome of the planting season as were the freedmen and demanded changes in the contract system. Already, in September of 1865, the state legislature had enacted a "black code" which, in effect, legally placed the position of the Negro midway between slavery and freedom. Among other things, the code granted broad authority to the white employer over his workers, and imposed upon the Negroes a number of severe restrictions, such as requiring them to work from sun to sun, to remain quiet at night, and not to leave the premises or receive visitors without permission of the owner.[16]

In many communities white landowners, through mass meetings and resolutions, sought to secure uniform practice among

12. Ralph Ely to Saxton, December 15, 1865, Bureau Records, S. C., Box 471.
13. Charleston *Courier*, November 25, 1865.
14. *Ibid.*, January 9, 1866.
15. Circular #2, December 2, 1865, Bureau Records, S. C., Box 473; Saxton to Ralph Ely, December 27, 1865, *ibid.*, Vol. 10.
16. See Simkins and Woody, *South Carolina During Reconstruction*, pp. 48-51.

their class. One such meeting, for example, adopted a form of contract whose demands upon the freedmen were appreciably more severe than the terms of Saxton's model agreement. Negro workers were to keep no poultry, dogs, firearms, or whiskey; further, they must agree to use care in the treatment of tools and animals, to pay for any negligent damage to either, and to keep their quarters in clean conditions. They were also to be required to perform a minimum amount of work per day in various areas: splitting rails, 125 to 150; cutting grain, 3 to 6 acres; hoeing cotton, 70 to 300 rows an acre long, etc. If work were to be assigned other than by task, the minimum workday was to consist of ten hours. For every involuntary absence each worker was to be fined fifty cents; for each willful absence, two dollars a day. If the laborer were absent more than once without permission, he subjected himself to dismissal and forfeiture of his share of the crops. In return for their labor, workers were to receive one-fourth of an acre each for their personal use and the privilege of getting firewood; they were also entitled to one-third of the net proceeds of the ginned cotton, following deductions of the cost of any rations advanced by the planter.[17]

In the upstate region the form of contract preferred by landowners followed this general pattern also, with the difference that most whites preferred to pay wages in money rather than shares of the crop, regarding this arrangement as a more effective means of controlling the Negro workers. The rate of pay usually averaged from eight to twelve dollars a month out of which, rather often, the Negro had to supply his own rations.[18]

Discouraged by such contract terms and persisting in their hope that they were still to get free farms of forty acres, many freedmen initially refused to accept labor agreements. In a few areas they displayed some signs of class-consciousness by organizing and resolving not to accept contracts until certain terms had been met; occasionally they managed to win acceptance of their demands. In at least one instance the Negro workers on a large plantation refused either to sign contracts or to leave the plantation, arming themselves to prevent forcible removal. Only a per-

17. Sumter *Watchman*, January 3 and 17, 1866. See also Sidney Andrews, *The South Since the War* (Boston, 1866), p. 206.

18. Newberry *Herald*, December 6, 1865; Charleston *Courier*, October 3, 1865; "Contracts," Greenville, Bureau Records, S. C., Vol. 209.

sonal appeal from General Scott led them, at length, to accept labor agreements for the year ahead.[19]

But in spite of such episodes, by March of 1866 an increasing number of Negroes were entering into labor agreements. In part this development had been brought about by an order from the Federal military commander of the state; while on the one hand it nullified the "black code" recently enacted by the state legislature, on the other it also declared that freedmen must enter into reasonable labor contracts within ten days or be removed by military force from the land.[20] In addition Bureau officials redoubled their efforts at arranging labor agreements in the early months of the new year. By the summer of 1866 agents had approved a total of about 8,000 contracts, embracing approximately 130,000 Negro workers.[21] Seemingly, the farming crisis for the year had passed.

The one conspicuous exception to the general pattern lay in the coastal area south of Charleston where, because the question of possessory titles to the land continued to agitate the minds of the freedmen, labor conditions remained unsettled. Most of the workers had eventually accepted contracts for the year, but, according to General Scott, refused to fulfill their terms. By late June he was concerned enough to issue a directive, noting "with deep regret" a spreading degree of "theft, drunkenness, and vagrancy" among the freedmen of the region. In the future, the order continued, any freedman wandering off the plantation in disregard of his contract terms was to be arrested and put to work on public roads; laborers refusing to accept labor contracts were to be forcibly removed from the land by Bureau officials. The assistant commissioner also admonished the Negroes to discontinue their practice of going in a body to the local Bureau agent to have some trivial matter arbitrated, thereby neglecting their work, and urged them to compose their own differences.[22]

Such strong words and stern measures apparently had some effect, for by late summer Negroes in this region, as well as in

19. D. T. Corbin to Scott, February 1, 1866, Bureau Records, S. C., Box 474; F. W. Leidtke to Scott, March 1, 1866, *ibid.*, Box 475; B. F. Smith to Scott, January 21, 1866, *ibid.*, Vol. 191; Beaufort *Weekly Republican*, January 20, 1866.
20. Charleston *Courier*, January 24, 1866.
21. Scott to Howard, November 1, 1866, Bureau Records, S. C., Vol. 11.
22. General Order #9, June 29, 1866, Bureau Records, S. C., Box 511.

other parts of the state, were reported to be working well. The Bureau, with the help of military forces, had reason for self-congratulation upon its contribution towards stability in the state's agricultural life. But by early autumn shadows were falling across the picture, as reports began to come from all parts of the state that told of discouraging prospect for the harvest. Widespread crop failures, resulting from a prolonged drought and the ravage of insects, were producing a general restlessness among both races. Agents reported that many planters, anticipating crop shortages, were driving the workers from the land before harvest time, and that many freedmen were neglecting their work because of what one described as "a succession of day huntings and night frolics" among them.[23] In an effort to prevent anarchy and to deal justly with both groups, General Scott announced the general Bureau policy in the situation. He warned the whites that plantations would be seized wherever the freedmen had been unjustly dismissed, and that the crops would be held for the exclusive benefit of the workers; he warned the Negroes that they would be forcibly ejected from the land and would have their wages forfeited if they failed to live up to the terms of their agreement.[24]

But such threats were futile in the face of the grim harvest prospects. It became increasingly clear that the planting season had been a dismal failure; neither in cotton nor food crops would production be great enough to support the planters and their workers during the year ahead. One agent accurately portrayed the situation when he remarked, "The share of the negro is eaten up by what has been advanced to him and the share of the employer barely replaces what he has advanced."[25]

Once more, as at the close of the previous year, many among both races felt frustrated over the results of the labor contract system and wanted changes introduced for 1867. An increasing number of landowners announced their intention to shift from a

23. John W. De Forest, *A Union Officer in the Reconstruction* (New Haven, 1948), p. 96. See also S. Place to Scott, July 25, 1866, Bureau Records, S. C., Box 545; W. K. Harkisheimer to Scott, August 31, 1866, *ibid.*, Vol. 132; G. W. Gile to Scott, August 31, 1866, *ibid.*, Box 519.

24. Scott to A. P. Carahar, August 11, 1866, and to D. T. Corbin, March 28, 1866, Bureau Records, S. C., Vol. 11.

25. J. W. De Forest to Scott, October 31, 1866, Bureau Records, S. C., Box 526. See also Yorkville *Inquirer*, August 9, 1866.

crop-sharing system to one of paying their workers in money wages, feeling that the latter would induce the freedmen to labor more industriously; they also announced their opposition to leasing land to Negroes, unless under direct white supervision, since such practice, in the words of one group, would produce "a state of things not only revolting to our natures but threatening to our existence."[26]

For their part, the freedmen had even more cause to be unhappy over the prevailing contract system. Large numbers had little or nothing to show for the year's labor, and some, in fact, were actually in debt because their share of the crops proved insufficient to pay for the rations that had been advanced by the planter. Moreover, among some the dream that a general land distribution would occur on New Year's Day lingered on. As a consequence, they refused in many localities to enter into labor agreements for the year ahead, leaving General Scott once more to threaten forcible removal from the plantations of those who refused to accept reasonable terms of labor. In some districts Negroes held popular meetings in an effort to find ways of improving their lot; in others, rather than be coerced into accepting distasteful conditions of employment, groups of them prepared to emigrate to Liberia or to the southwest where homestead land was available. But the great majority eventually compromised with the inevitable and accepted the contracts that were offered by the whites. By late spring reports indicated that the contract system was in operation in most regions of the state on a pattern essentially similar to that of 1866, and that generally the freedmen were working well.[27]

Yet the promise of spring was not fulfilled by the months that followed. The summer of 1867 proved, at least figuratively, to be long and hot as a result of the launching of the congressional program of Reconstruction. Since the program reorganized the civil affairs of the state and enfranchised eligible freedmen, it inevitably affected the relationship of white employers and their Negro workers. Most of the whites bitterly resented the Radical

26. Fairfield *Herald*, October 10, 1866; Sumter *Watchman*, September 5, 1866; and Charleston *Mercury*, January 3, 1867.

27. Charleston *Courier*, November 4 and 17, 1866, and February 15, 1867; Charleston *Daily News*, February 27 and May 21, 1866; J. W. De Forest to Scott, January 31, 1867, Bureau Records, S. C., Box 526; J. M. Johnston to Scott, December 15, 1866, *ibid.*, Box 475.

Reconstruction measures, especially that which armed the ex-slaves with the ballot; and they were further angered when Negroes began flocking to the polls to register and later to vote, often at the price of neglecting the growing crops. In many cases this anger was raised to white heat by the energetic and successful efforts of Union League clubs in preaching the gospel of staunch Republicanism to the Negro voters. Before the summer was over, racial tension was mounting and, in some areas, exploding into physical violence.

An additional factor which helped further to unsettle relations between the planters and the freedmen was the increasing prospect that crop shortages were going to be even more severe than in 1866. A prolonged drought, followed by exceptionally heavy rains, had seriously damaged the growing crops, creating the distinct possibility that both employers and workers would get smaller returns than they had the year before. Many of the landowners, according to complaints of the freedmen that deluged Bureau offices throughout the fall, were driving the Negroes off the land to avoid paying them their rightful share of the crops; many of the workers, according to numerous complaints of the whites, were wandering off to search for other work, in utter disregard of their contracts. Bureau officials were constantly besieged by demands from each side that the other be compelled to honor the terms of the labor agreements.[28]

Once the crops were harvested, it was all too clear that the growing season had been a disastrous failure. Those freedmen who had worked for a share of the crops suffered especially. Typical of hundreds of others was the case of twenty-two freedmen who had worked on a crop-sharing arrangement. The share of each for the entire year amounted to $24.70; but after the cost of rations advanced by the planter was deducted, seven of them found they had a net income of from four to eight dollars, and the remaining fifteen found themselves indebted to the planter for amounts that ranged from two to sixty dollars.[29] An experienced officer of the Bureau, commenting upon the situation

28. J. B. Dennis to Scott, July 7, 1867, Bureau Records, S. C., Box 511; Robert Beckett to Scott, July 4, 1867, ibid., Vol. 228; George Pingree to Scott, September 24, 1867, ibid., Vol. 177.

29. E. W. Everson to Scott, May 11, 1868, Bureau Records, S. C., Vol. 44.

in his region, declared: "At no period since the close of the War has this District been in such an utterly destitute and helpless condition."[30]

Most of the whites were hardly any better off. The year had been as unkind to them, in many ways, as to the freedmen. But in surveying the wreckage of the planting season, many of them tended to ignore the role played by nature and instead to place the blame upon the Negro. One spokesman asserted that the two successive years of crop failure had been "the inevitable results of worthless labor, paid extraordinary wages and allowed unheard of privileges;" the solution, he went on, must come from the whites' recognizing that "the duty we owe our country and our race demands that we do all we can to keep . . . [the freedmen] in a real state of dependence upon us, first, for food and raiment, then for such privileges as we may deem proper to accord."[31] Other spokesmen believed that the main cause of crop failures lay in the Negroes' neglect of their work to attend political gatherings, a charge partially supported by the observation of one Bureau official that he had found Negroes "traveling ten and twenty miles to League meetings and, what with coming and going, making a three days' job of it, leaving the weeds to take care of the corn."[32] Still others placed the blame at the doorstep of the Bureau. One newspaper editor, for example, declared: "Among the many misfortunes of the poor South, is the fact that her little remaining substance is consumed, and the people . . . plundered by a vast horde of swindling adventurers, Bureau agents and officers, who cover the earth like locusts."[33]

Out of the failure and frustration of the year came not only a heightening of ill-will between planter and worker but also an effort by a number of white groups to supply their labor needs with European immigrants in place of Negro workers. Planter societies were formed, money was raised, and agents were sent abroad in search of laborers willing to immigrate to the state. Though a few hundred Europeans were induced to make the

30. Scott to Howard, February 28, 1868, Bureau Records, S. C., Vol. 44.
31. "Marion," Orangeburg *News,* January 4, 1868.
32. De Forest, *A Union Officer,* pp. 99-100; John B. Dennis to Scott, July 7, 1867, Bureau Records, S. C., Vol. 228; George Pingree to Scott, September 24, 1867, *ibid.,* Vol. 177.
33. Anderson *Intelligencer,* January 29, 1868. See also the Charleston *Daily News,* December 12, 1867.

venture, no large number responded and in the end the movement failed.[34]

For their part, a number of freedmen once more sought to
escape from their distress by moving to the southwest in search
of homestead land; reliable estimates placed at thirty-seven thousand the number who had left the state for Mississippi and Texas
since 1865.[35] Of those who remained behind, some sought once
more through organized effort to secure a bettering of their lot
by demanding contracts with more generous terms for themselves. Still others simply refused to enter into labor agreements,
probably because of a lingering hope that at New Year's the
long hoped-for distribution of land would still take place.[36] So
widespread was their refusal in the coastal area that General
Scott felt compelled to issue a circular announcing that workers
who would not accept labor contracts "must leave the plantations
and give up the quarters which they now occupy to such
workers as are willing to contract." He added: "If they refuse
to quietly leave, military force will be used to remove them." He
also warned that no Bureau rations would be issued to those who
refused to accept labor contracts.[37]

Eventually, as it became clear that they were not to get forty-
acre farms, most of the freedmen accepted labor contracts for the
new year. Under such circumstances economic necessity was
far more important than any policy of the Bureau in determining
the Negroes' working condition. No number of announcements
from Scott's headquarters, no amount of effort by his subordinates, could do much to solve the cause of distress among both
races, or substantially to alter the racial prejudice of the whites
towards the Negro, especially after his enfranchisement by the
Radical Reconstruction program. Thus the position of most
freedmen for 1868 came to be defined more by the law of economic and social relationship than by any action by the Bureau.
Scott must surely have voiced the frustration of many of his subordinates when, a full three years after the close of the War, he

34. Simkins and Woody, *South Carolina During Reconstruction*, pp.
243-47.

35. Henry Latham, *Black and White* (London, 1867), p. 269.

36. W. H. Holton to Scott, January 10 and 30, 1868, Bureau Records,
S. C., Vol. 253; W. H. Evans to George Pingree, January 21, 1868, *ibid.*,
Box 519; J. E. Lewis to Scott, January 31, 1868, *ibid.*, Vol. 212.

37. Circular #2, January 9, 1867, Bureau Records, S. C., Vol. 26.

sarcastically sympathized with a white who complained that his Negro worker had broken his contract to seek work elsewhere. "Four dollars a month," he wrote the planter, "with 2½ pounds of bacon and one peck of meal per week, and only $1 per day deducted for absences without leave and 25¢ per day . . . on account of sickness is surely all that any able-bodied man should ask for . . . doing all kinds of work . . . from sunrise to dusk." With contempt he added, "I am not surprised that you should feel greatly outraged that this man has been induced to withdraw from a contract so liberal and just."[38]

Yet in spite of such exceptional contracts as the one Scott referred to, as the year advanced prospects brightened that 1868 would be a year of better returns for both Negroes and whites. For one thing, a measure of political stability returned to the state's affairs following the establishment of a new civil government. For another, favorable weather conditions prevailed throughout the growing season, helping to produce a harvest that was the best and largest of the postwar period. Planters and freedmen alike enjoyed more substantial returns for the year's labor and thus were able more confidently to face the new growing season ahead.[39]

It was on this brighter note that the Bureau, at the end of 1868, closed out its operation and thus ended its four-year effort to organize and develop a free labor system in the state. The task it had faced in trying to define and regulate the new relationship between ex-master and ex-slave had been immense. The aftermath of war, the unsettled condition of large numbers of freedmen, the unwillingness of the whites to accord the Negro his status of full freedom, the adversities of the weather, and the political climate created by the Radical Reconstruction program, all had played a part in creating a social and economic question beyond the capabilities of the Bureau to solve, especially in light of its restricted personnel and limited life.

At best, it could have provided only a partial solution, as both races groped their way through the strange and new adjustment of free white and free Negro, without precedent or experience to guide them. And this much, at least, the agency did

38. Scott to J. V. Nether, April 10, 1868, Bureau Records, S. C., Vol. 13.
39. J. R. Edie to Howard, October 19, 1868, Bureau Records, S. C., Vol. 13.

accomplish. Even white spokesmen admitted, from time to time, that the free labor system was proving a qualified success. At the end of 1866, for example, Governor James L. Orr told the legislature in his annual message that the new system, while not wholly satisfactory, was "far from proving a failure. Where the blacks have been adequately compensated and kindly treated, they have generally labored faithfully."[40] A number of newspapers, in the following year, echoed a similar sentiment about the performance of the Negro workers.[41] That the Bureau is entitled to a sizable share of the credit for such results seems entirely clear.

Moreover, there is abundant evidence to suggest that the whites in 1865, had they been left to their own judgment, would have fixed the status of the Negro at some point short of the full freedom to which he was entitled. The presence and work of the Bureau undoubtedly helped to insure a fuller justice and fairer treatment to the Negro laborer; and even if, at the close of 1868, he was still far from knowing adequate economic security, at least the Bureau had contributed towards establishing the simple yet cardinal truth that he *was* a free worker, entitled to bargain for the terms of his labor.

Moreover, the Bureau had endeavored to instruct the Negro in his responsibilities as a free worker, especially during the two and a half years of Scott's leadership. Again and again, Scott and his subordinates had cautioned the freedmen about the necessity of fulfilling their labor contracts; and the recorded instances in which the Bureau used force against recalcitrant or irresponsible freedmen are at least as numerous as those in which it was used against dishonest planters. It should be remembered, finally, that both races would have suffered a much greater distress during the crop failures of 1867 but for the Bureau's program of advancing rations on crop-lien security. Only through such assistance were thousands of whites and Negroes enabled to survive until the following harvest.

At the end of 1868, when the Bureau ceased its operations, the system of contract labor which it had worked to create was still

40. *Message No. 1 of His Excellency Governor J. L. Orr* (Columbia, 1866), p. 9.
41. Columbia *Daily Phoenix*, June 18, 1867; Orangeburg *News*, April 20, 1867.

far short of perfection. The great majority of Negro workers were hardly any better off materially than they had been under slavery. Nevertheless, the Bureau had helped to establish the principle that, as a free man, the Negro laborer had certain rights and privileges, and to compel white employers to recognize this principle. If, as was the case, the Negro worker by 1869 was a few steps closer to the fulfillment of freedom, the Bureau must receive at least partial credit as the agency which made the difficult path a little easier for his weary feet to travel.

Of the many efforts of the Bureau in South Carolina to uplift the freedmen, none was accompanied by more excitement or marked by greater fervor than its work in the realm of education where, from the beginning, the Negroes displayed a burning eagerness for schooling. They may not have understood perfectly the abstraction of freedom, but they strongly sensed that there was meaning to be found in solving the mystery of the written word. Nor was this feeling confined to any one group or any particular region. Observers everywhere reported that the young and old, from far and near, were flocking to attend the newly-created schools. Intuitively, the freedmen seemed to know that in this strange world of words and letters lay a power capable of moving them along the road of freedom. Something of their fervor was expressed in the story told by a young teacher working among them. "We notice," she related, "that all the children and grownups also hold their books sidewise; when we asked why, a man answered, 'We wish to learn to read on all sides.' "[1]

This zeal of the freedmen to learn was equalled, and sometimes surpassed, by that of the teachers to teach. Responding to the call of churches and benevolent societies, young women and men from all parts of the North, and especially from New England, came to teach in the Negro schools that were being established in South Carolina, as elsewhere throughout the South. Many took up the work in a spirit not unlike that of the medieval knight assuming the crusader's vow. They entered upon it not alone to rescue the freedman from his ignorance, but also to redeem the South from her sins of the past, to make the region, in the words of one of their spokesmen, a place that would be safe for "the reddest Republican" or "the blackest Abolition-

1. Mary Ames, *From a New England Woman's Diary in Dixie in 1865* (Springfield, 1906), p. 55.

ist."[2] Many of those who entered teaching were moved to do so by a deep, and sometimes overwrought, emotionalism about the plight of the former slaves. Typical was one who likened the teacher's mission to that of Moses with the Hebrew children. It was an inexpressible experience, she wrote, to be among the freedmen "as their morning dawns; to see them personally, coming forth from the land of Egypt and the house of bondage. . . . It is a joy and a glory for which there are not words."[3]

Such strong emotionalism, though not insincere, in many cases did prove to be insubstantial. Those teachers whose zeal exceeded their conviction soon wearied of the venture, once the novelty and excitement were gone, and returned to the North, dispirited and sometimes disillusioned about the nature of the undertaking. But there were others whose commitment to the cause of Negro schooling was both deep and lasting; they were individuals who brought to the movement dignity and nobility through their willingness to forswear a life of security and comfort for one of sacrifice and physical hardship. Foremost among such persons in South Carolina were women like Martha Schofield, a Pennsylvanian who came to this state in 1866 and gave the next forty-eight years of her life to Negro education, founding at the city of Aiken an institution still in existence; Laura M. Towne, who devoted thirty-eight years to the cause; Rachel Mather, who spent thirty-five years in the field; and Abby D. Monroe, who served for over four decades as director of the Laing School for freedmen in Mt. Pleasant.[4] The discomforts they endured ranged from such inconveniences as broken windows, leaking roofs and sharing their quarters with uninvited rattlesnakes to such tribulations as verbal abuse and physical threats from hostile whites.[5] It was persons such as these who

2. Henry L. Swint, *The Northern Teacher in the South, 1862-1870* (Nashville, 1941), p. 58.

3. *Ibid.,* p. 41.

4. Miss Schofield founded the Schofield Normal and Industrial Institute at Aiken, Miss Towne the Penn School of St. Helena. Matilda Evans, *Martha Schofield: Pioneer Negro Educator* (Columbia, 1916), pp. 17-33; Francis B. Simkins and Robert H. Woody, *South Carolina During Reconstruction* (Chapel Hill, 1932), p. 430; L. P. Jackson, "The Educational Efforts of the Freedmen's Bureau and the Freedmen's Aid Societies in South Carolina, 1862-1872," *Journal of Negro History,* VIII (1923), 1-40.

5. Ames, *New England Woman's Diary,* pp. 17-18, 49, 108-9; Swint, *Northern Teacher,* pp. 77-80.

gave strength, purpose, and high resolve to the movement to lift the pall of ignorance from the former slaves.

Another person who deserves mention for doing more than yeoman's service in the cause, despite the political controversy that would later swirl around him, was B. F. Whittemore. A native of Massachusetts and a graduate of Amherst, he was a Methodist minister before the war who became a chaplain in a Massachusetts regiment during the conflict and who found himself in South Carolina at war's end. In the summer of 1865 he was named by General Saxton as assistant superintendent of education for eastern South Carolina, a region of eight counties with a total Negro population of about one hundred thousand. At the time of his appointment Whittemore found not a single school for Negroes in existence throughout his entire district. With funds so limited that he sometimes had to pay expenses from his personal means, he set about the task of building a school system by using barns and huts for classrooms and former slaves with some education as teachers. By the following spring he had managed, with the help of the New England Freedmen's Commission, to organize 13 schools with an enrollment of 1100 and a teaching staff of 14. From then until the Bureau's disbandment in the state, he labored with energy and with dedication to improve and enlarge the system he had established.[6]

The task of recruiting the teachers and financing the movement fell mainly to the benevolent societies and church organizations in the North rather than to the Bureau. Of these the most prominent were the Freedmen's Union Commission, a non-sectarian group founded in 1863, and the American Missionary Association, established originally in 1846 as an anti-slavery organization. In addition, every major Protestant Church sponsored and supported one or more institutions of learning for Negroes.[7]

6. C. H. Howard to Saxton, November 29, 1865, Bureau Records, S. C., Box 488; Whittemore to Scott, April 17 and May 25, 1866, ibid., Box 476, and January 1, March 28, 1867, ibid., Box 479; Charleston Daily News, March 9, 1868. Another who labored with dedication against great odds was T. G. Wright, in the region around Columbia. A. A. Taylor, The Negro in South Carolina During Reconstruction (Washington, 1924), pp. 90-91.

7. J. H. Parmelee, Freedmen's Aid Societies, 1861-1871, U. S. Department of Interior, Bulletin 38 (Washington, 1917); G. K. Eggleston, "The Work of Relief Societies During the Civil War," Journal of Negro History, XIV (1929), 272-99; Ralph Morrow, "Northern Methodism in the South

The movement thus was one sustained mainly by private, not public, benevolence. Yet the role of the Bureau in promoting Negro education, while secondary, was nevertheless real. Though it did not recruit or hire the teachers, it did perform other needed functions, among them the investigation of school needs, the co-ordination of the work of the various societies, and the publicizing of the cause and progress of Negro education before the nation. It also used a considerable portion of its funds, under congressional authorization, for "the repair and rental" of school buildings—a phrase construed with great liberality by Bureau officials to provide the greatest possible assistance to Negro schooling.

The beginnings of the educational crusade in South Carolina can be traced to 1862 when, as part of the Sea Island Experiment, the Reverend Solomon Peck of Boston opened a school for freedmen at Beaufort. From then until war's close the number of schools grew steadily as Federal forces gradually expanded their area of control. All told, by the summer of 1865 more than nine thousand Negro children were enrolled in schools along the coastal region.[8] Thus, when the Bureau began actual operations in the state it found the nucleus of an educational system already functioning. Reuben Tomlinson, a civilian of considerable experience with the Sea Island Experiment, became superintendent of the Bureau's educational division in the state and undertook the task of enlarging and improving the system he found in operation. In his very first circular, after requesting that people inform him of school needs in their locality, he announced the aim of the educational endeavor: "The purpose of this . . . branch . . . is neither to destroy nor unnecessarily to interfere, but simply to assist in repairing the 'waste places,' and in laying sure the foundations of future happiness and greatness of the people."[9] From the beginning he worked steadily to expand the

During Reconstruction," *Mississippi Valley Historical Review*, XLI (1954), 413-40.

8. Guion Johnson, *A Social History of the Sea Islands* (Chapel Hill, 1930), pp. 154-215; Elizabeth W. Pearson (ed.), *Letters from Port Royal* (Boston,1906), pp. 5-7; Bell Wiley, *Southern Negroes, 1861-1865* (New Haven, 1938), Chap. XIV; Willie Lee Rose, *Rehearsal for Reconstruction: The Port Royal Experiment* (Indianapolis, 1964), Chap. VIII.

9. Charleston *Courier*, October 19, 1865. Biographical data on Tomlinson came from the following: Saxton to Howard, August 14, 1865, Bu-

system into all parts of the state. By the summer of 1866 he could report that 54 schools were in operation with a teaching staff of 130. Student enrollment was nearly 8,000 and average daily attendance about 5,500. In addition, an indeterminate number of night schools were providing some kind of basic instruction to adults. Tomlinson estimated—probably with some exaggeration—that at least 30,000 Negroes had learned to read during the previous school year.[10]

It was the superintendent's hope during the new academic year of 1866-1867 to improve the program, not only through expansion but also by closer co-ordination of effort among the benevolent societies. He sought to have each society instruct its teachers to report to his office on such things as the location and size of each school, length of the academic term, program of studies, classification of students by grade, and also about the climate of white opinion in the vicinity towards Negro education. But he never succeeded in getting full co-operation from the teachers. Some simply ignored his request for information; others refused on the ground that they were not subject to the jurisdiction of the Bureau.[11] Consequently, Tomlinson never knew with accuracy the number of schools in operation or the number of Negro children enrolled in them. Another problem which arose to obstruct his efforts came from the rivalry that sometimes developed among the societies themselves. In one instance, for example, factionalism among three different Methodist groups grew so pronounced that it became impossible to secure any unity of action among their rival Negro congregations in behalf of schooling. In a second case the Freedmen's Union Commission objected strenuously when another benevolent society, with the Bureau's help, sought to establish a school in the same city as the Commission's.[12]

Yet in spite of such problems, Tomlinson remained optimistic about the prospects for the new year, heartened especially by

reau Records, S. C., Vol. 9; Charleston *Courier,* October 6, 1865; *The Nation,* I (December 21, 1865), 770.

10. Tomlinson to Scott, May 6, July 7, and November 3, 1866, Bureau Records, Box 1098.

11. Many of the printed forms are in Box 491, Bureau Records, S. C.

12. Tomlinson to Scott, October 9, 1866, Bureau Records, S. C., Box 476; H. H. Griffin to E. L. Deane, November 18, 1869, *ibid.,* Box 490; Freedmen's Union Commission to Howard, May 1, 1869, *ibid.,* Box 482.

the increase in funds at his disposal from the appropriation provided the Bureau by Congress in 1866. Another cause for optimism lay in the continuing enthusiasm of the freedmen for education; indeed they were, if possible, even more avid for schooling than ever. By the thousands children flocked to the schools as they opened and the parents, from their meager means, contributed in goods and money twice as much to the support of the schools during 1866-1867 as they had in the year before.

One example of the dedication given by the freedmen to schooling might be found in the case of Charles Hopkins in the city of Greenville. A former slave who had managed to gain the rudiments of an education, he was determined, with the coming of freedom, to do something to foster learning among his own race. Without property or other resources save his character, he managed to raise about two hundred dollars in contributions from the whites of the city and then to borrow an additional three hundred dollars. With this sum he rented a plot of land, enlisted the help of fellow freedmen in dismantling and reconstructing an old warehouse on it, and opened a school for Negro children of the area. Handicapped by a shortage of money and badgered by his creditors, he labored alone for several months to keep the school alive until at length, with the timely aid of the Bureau, he succeeded in hiring a teaching staff of five and developing an enrollment of three hundred. In time he managed to transform the school into one of the best in the state, according to the testimony of Superintendent Tomlinson.[13]

The dedicated labor of Hopkins, though perhaps exceptional in its degree, was not unusual. Wherever schools were in operation, Negroes responded enthusiastically to the chance to learn. Tomlinson wrote in June of 1867 that the freedmen, from their very limited means, were contributing towards the support of nearly one-third of the Negro schools in the state. He also reported that during the year, according to official figures submitted to his office, 73 schools had been in operation, with a teaching staff of 140 and an enrollment of about 8,000. He esti-

13. John W. De Forest, *A Union Officer in the Reconstruction* (New Haven, 1948), pp. 118-21; De Forest to Scott, December 31, 1866, Bureau Records, S. C., Box 526; Tomlinson to Scott, March 26, 1868, *ibid.*, Box 481.

mated that, in addition, at least 40 unreported institutions with a teaching staff of 60 and an enrollment of 4,000 students had operated. A total of $107,000 had been spent in the state for Negro education during the 1866-67 school year, of which the Bureau had contributed about $25,000 for "rental and repair" needs, benevolent societies about $65,000, and the freedmen themselves nearly $17,000.[14]

Such figures gave Tomlinson and the other friends of Negro education cause for encouragement, since in every case the statistics revealed greater support for the movement than in the previous year. Yet there was also cause for concern. Even if the most liberal allowance is made for the number of students enrolled in unreported schools and night classes, not more than 25,000 Negro children of school age were in any way involved in education. In other words, from the whole school-age population among Negroes of about 125,000, four out of every five children were not even so much as nominally touched by the educational program in the state.[15] Yet Tomlinson, in planning for the new school term ahead, viewed such statistics more as a challenge than as a cause for discouragement. The freedmen themselves, moreover, remained as zealous as ever for schooling, the old not less than the young. A foreign observer, touring the South, recorded that the "great and crowning desire" of Negro adults was to acquire enough education to be able to read the Bible. Said one of them, who had begun to master the rudiments of reading: "It's so sweet to pick out dis verse and dat verse, and tink 'dem's the 'dentical words my Saviour spoke.' "[16]

But neither the determination of the superintendent nor the zeal of the freedmen could overcome certain harsh and stubborn facts. The new school term of 1867-1868 had hardly begun before the clear truth emerged that it was going to be even less successful than the previous year in the number of schools in operation and the size of student enrollment. The drop appears to have been caused by several factors. The inauguration of the Radical Reconstruction program in the summer of 1867 did much to create a climate of discord in the state which had an

14. Tomlinson to Scott, July 1, 1867, Bureau Records, Box 1098.
15. The figure of 125,000 is based upon the estimate of J. W. Alvord, *Letters from the South Relating to the Freedmen* (Washington, 1870), V, 47.
16. David Macrae, *The Americans at Home* (New York, 1952), p. 296.

adverse effect on the progress of Negro schooling. Moreover, severe crop failures that fall made it even more difficult for Negro parents to contribute towards the support of schools or to get along without the labor of their children on the farms.[17] Finally, a declining interest in the North towards education for the Southern freedmen, as well as a loss of enthusiasm among some of the missionary educators themselves, caused the private societies to reduce their support of schools. Inevitably, the statistics at the close of the term in the summer of 1868 reflected the decline. Tomlinson reported that the average number of schools known by his office to be in operation during the academic year had been only 49 (in contrast to the 73 of the previous year), with an average number of 123 teachers. Enrollment of students had been nearly 7,000 and average attendance over 5,000. He estimated that, in addition, at least 8,000 children were attending schools which had not reported to his office, meaning that almost 15,000 pupils were getting some kind of classroom instruction. He also estimated that a total of $127,000 had been spent on Negro education in the state during the year, of which the Bureau had contributed $57,000.[18]

It became apparent in the new school term 1868-1869 that the curtailment of the previous year was as much prophecy for the future as summary of the past. As events soon proved, the educational movement had reached and passed its peak. Northern societies slackened still further their support of education; Tomlinson resigned as superintendent to accept a state office under Governor Scott, thereby removing his experienced leadership at a time when it was still critically needed; and the Bureau, as its remaining funds dwindled, found itself compelled to reduce its assistance to the program. By the end of the year much of the momentum of the movement had been lost. Total school enrollment had dropped to about 5,500 and average attendance to about 4,500. The Bureau superintendent reported that 54 schools had been in operation, but since he included an unspecified number of Sunday Schools (which sometimes offered some elementary instruction) in this figure, there is no way of knowing just how many of the schools had been regular institutions.[19]

17. Tomlinson to Scott, July 1, 1868, Bureau Records, Box 1098.
18. *Ibid.*
19. Howard to Scott, July 31, 1868, Bureau Records, S. C., Box 481; J.

Nevertheless, it is clear that the total was appreciably less than in the preceding term. The tide was unmistakably receding.

The following year witnessed the end of the Bureau's support of Negro education, since by the summer of 1870 its funds for education were exhausted. At the same time private societies further curtailed their support because, as one discouraged teacher wrote, the people of the North "have got tired of giving."[20] Though the new state government established under the congressional plan of reconstruction had drawn up an ambitious plan for public schooling, the Bureau's superintendent of education was highly dubious that the blueprint would be translated into reality. And this skepticism, together with the growing apathy in the North about further support of schools for freedmen, filled him with deep misgivings about the future of Negro education in the state. In documenting his pessimism he noted that, for one thing, economic necessity would continue to force Negro children after a few years of rudimentary learning to drop out of school to aid the family in earning a livelihood. For another, he went on, the great majority of the men serving as county commissioners of education—an office recently established by the state legislature—were incompetent, illiterate, or ignorant. Finally, he observed, white opinion in the state towards Negro schooling appeared more hostile in 1870 than ever. He concluded by writing gloomily that "so much is daily said upon the dark side of this matter, that it is not pleasant for me to dwell upon it. I consequently do not feel willing to continue this communication further."[21]

It was on this note that the Bureau brought to a close its educational endeavor in South Carolina. Its funds exhausted, it proceeded to dispose of all its school property—some 50 buildings valued at $75,000—to the private societies for their use in support of Negro schooling. According to the superintendent's final report

R. Edie to Howard, October 19, 1868, *ibid.*, Vol. 13; "Schools Supported by Private Associations, 1868," *ibid.*, Vol. 47 and Box 490; Reports of Horace Niede, February and May, 1869, *ibid.*, Box 490.

20. Cornelia Hancock to E. L. Deane, March 4, 1870, Bureau Records, S. C., Box 490. See also the letters to Deane from M. R. Miller, April 11, 1870, and Martha Schofield, May 6, 1870, *ibid.*, Box 490; Deane to Howard, June 30, 1870, Bureau Records, Box 1099.

21. E. L. Deane to Howard, March 1, 1870, and January 20, 1870, Bureau Records, Box 1098.

of July 15, 1870, a total of 86 schools, with a teaching staff of nearly 200 and an enrollment of almost 9,000, had been in operation during the previous year.[22] But in light of the factors discussed above, it seems inconceivable that the number of private schools could have been greater in 1870 than in 1869. In giving the total the superintendent apparently did not bother to distinguish between the schools maintained by private support and those recently established by state authority; the former, in all probability, numbered no more than half the reported figure.

Statistics themselves tell much about the size and scope of the educational endeavor of the Bureau and the benevolent groups during the five years between 1865 and 1870, but they tell nothing of the nature of the school program itself. In most cases the schools established under Northern auspices sought to reproduce for their Negro students a course of studies patterned after that prevailing in the schools of the North. It was, on the one hand, a curriculum concerned with substance and content, with moral maxims, and with promoting mental and social discipline; it was, on the other, one that included subjects wholly foreign to the experience, and often alien to the needs of, children so recently come from bondage. In addition to the three R's and some religious instruction, the program included courses in the geography of Europe, Asia, and South America, history, physiology, natural philosophy, Latin, and classical literature. Apart from the practical uses implicit in the three R's, some schools also included a vocational course or two in such areas as sewing, but vocationalism always remained of minor importance.[23] The result was that the educational system introduced the Negro student to the world of learning without realistically introducing him to the world in which he had to live. It was, on the whole, a program more suited to the needs of a socially proficient people than to the needs of one just emerging from slavery; it also failed to recognize that neither in her society, her economy, nor her cultural tradition was South Carolina the counterpart of Massachusetts. A foreign traveler in the state offered perhaps the most apt judgment when he concluded that the schooling being given

22. E. L. Deane to Howard, July 15, 1870, Bureau Records, Box 1098.
23. These observations are drawn from innumerable reports of teachers concerning the courses of study offered. For many examples of them see Box 491 of Bureau Records, S. C.

the freedmen was training them "for the situation of a clerk, or for keeping a shop" but hardly at all for improving their lot in the agrarian world in which they lived.[24]

The schools themselves ranged in caliber from superior to miserable. One of the best was Avery Institute in Charleston, founded in 1865 by the American Missionary Association and headed by Francis L. Cardoza, a free-born mulatto of Charleston who was a man of exceptional educational background.[25] Another was the Penn School Number One of St. Helena, directed by Laura M. Towne and supported by the Pennsylvania branch of the Freedman's Union Commission. Under her able leadership the Negro students made remarkable progress in their knowledge of arithmetic, reading, writing, geography, American history, and civics; her system of discipline, which apparently was quite successful, made no use of corporal punishment but instead secured its effect by an elaborate system of honors and rewards, along with such punishment as detaining the student after school and requiring him to write a fixed amount of work.[26] A third was the Franklin Street School of Charleston, which had been established largely through the efforts of A. Toomer Porter, an Episcopal rector of the city who succeeded in getting a sizable financial support from Northern individuals for the enterprise. With a teaching staff of twelve native Carolinians and an enrollment of eight hundred, the school developed an instructional program that was standard in nature, along with a disciplinary system that was exceptional in its demands. A student who was tardy to class was given a number of demerits; if he were absent a total of ten or more days, whatever the cause, his class grade was lowered one rank; if he were absent ten consecutive days without permission he was expelled; if in his work he fell below the general average of the class, he was demoted to the grade below; and if he were insubordinate or willfully disobedient, he was immediately dismissed.[27]

24. F. Barham Zineke, *Last Winter in the United States* (London, 1868), pp. 102-3.

25. Tomlinson to Scott, July 1, 1867, Bureau Records, Box 1098; Francis B. Simkins and Robert H. Woody, *South Carolina During Reconstruction* (Chapel Hill, 1932), pp. 116-17; Macrae, *Americans at Home*, p. 266.

26. Tomlinson to Scott, July 1, 1868, Bureau Records, Box 1098.

27. Kate Savage to E. L. Deane, June 30, 1870, Bureau Records, S. C.,

At the opposite end of the scale in quality were the numerous one-room schools which were often held in barns and sheds. Not infrequently they were taught by teachers whose learning barely surpassed that of their students, as a letter from one of them in Edgefield suggests. Dated "ferbury 15" at "Edg field destrict," it read: ". . . I am teachen Still at the ridge al tho I ant at the Same place. . . . the bush whackers says I Should not keep School thare . . . So Have move my School 3 mils from thare. . . . thair wars but one name as I heard of that wars a ganst me and thar fore it looke quare and if no acedent takes place I will con tin ure here al the year."[28] One wonders whether, under such a teacher, the cause of education was advanced very far.

A final factor bearing upon the educational endeavor of the Bureau and the benevolent societies during their five-year joint effort was the attitude of whites towards Negro schooling—a matter about which no simple or easy generalization can be made. There was never any concerted or systematic effort by the whites to prevent the establishment of schools for the freedmen, though from time to time and place to place opposition did flare up. Late in 1865 Superintendent Tomlinson reported that there existed "a settled determination" by the whites that the freedmen "cannot and therefore *must* not be educated."[29] Reports from his subordinates in various parts of the state, both then and later, spoke of white hostility which sometimes assumed an ugly form. On occasion school buildings were burned and the teachers subjected to verbal abuse or physical violence from white natives. A number of agents reported that in their region the maintenance of Negro schools was made possible only by the presence of Federal troops in the locality.[30] Occasionally, hostile whites achieved their purpose by less direct means than force. In the little

---

Box 490. Another of high caliber was the Howard School in Columbia, established in 1867 under the auspices of the New York branch of the Freedmen's Union Commission. Columbia *Daily Phoenix*, June 25, 1868.

28. Elizabeth Dogget to William Stone, February 15, 1868, Bureau Records, S. C., Box 502.

29. Tomlinson to Saxton, November 22, 1865, Bureau Records, S. C., Box 487.

30. Samplings of the many reports telling of white abuse and threats towards teachers can be found in the following: Tomlinson to Scott, July 7, 1866, Bureau Records, Box 1098; B. F. Whittemore to Saxton, December 30, 1865, Bureau Records, S. C., Box 473; George Gile to Scott, May 18, 1866, *ibid.*, Vol. 175; Benjamin Runkle to Scott, October 12, 1866, *ibid.*,

mountain town of Walhalla, for example, the Methodist Episcopal Church had established a school under the direction of a young lady from Vermont. Within weeks local citizens had broken it up and driven the teacher away by hiring a vagabond Negro drunkard to attend her classes and to dog her steps daily through the streets.[31]

Yet during the same period of time in which white opposition to Negro schooling was making itself felt, numerous instances of white encouragement and support to the movement were occurring. As early as 1865, for example, the Charleston board of commission was seeking ways and means of implementing its resolution which had expressed a "sense of importance" in providing education for the Negro children of the city and its desire "of contributing to the promotion of this desirable object."[32] Out of this move came the ultimate establishment, under city auspices, of the Morris Street School, the only instance in the state in which municipal authorities voluntarily assumed the support of a Negro institution.[33] In another case the state Baptist Convention went on record as recommending education of freed children.[34] In still other instances Negro schools received support from some towns which offered vacant buildings for school purposes, from planters who gave land and lumber, and from other white citizens who donated land and money to be used in the cause.[35] Newspapers sometimes spoke out in behalf of the movement, as did the *Daily Phoenix* of Columbia in commending the work being done at the Howard School for Negroes in that city. The more education which the freedmen acquired,

---

Vol. 91; William Stone to L. Walker, June 1, 1868, *ibid.*, Box 521; Scott to Howard, August 14, 1868, *ibid.*, Vol. 13.

31. E. L. Deane to Howard, January 20, 1870, Bureau Records, Box 1098.

32. Tomlinson to Saxton, November 22, 1865, Bureau Records, S. C., Box 487.

33. Burchill R. Moore, "A History of Negro Public Schools of Charleston, South Carolina, 1867-1942" (Master's thesis, University of South Carolina, 1942), p. 6.

34. *Keowee Courier*, August 11, 1866.

35. Typical instances of white support of Negro schools can be found in: William Stone to John Devereaux, April 1, 1866, Bureau Records, S. C., Box 521; William Stone to T. G. Wright, July 13, 1866, *ibid.*, Vol. 106; T. G. Wright to Ralph Ely, December 7, 1865, *ibid.*, Box 518; Samuel Place to Scott, September 22, 1866, *ibid.*, Box 518; Tomlinson to Scott, July 7, 1866, Bureau Records, Box 1098.

wrote the editor, "the more they will add of assistance in the common development of our resources. In addition to these considerations, we desire to see the freedmen enjoy all the advantages of judicious education, and this is the feeling of all the right-minded persons in our community."[36] Moreover, the white community appears to have attached no social stigma to the teaching of freedmen by native whites. In dozens of cases white Carolinians, including several ex-Confederate soldiers, became teachers in Negro schools. To cite but a few of many examples, in Anderson three native whites were engaged in teaching Negro children; in Kershaw County, of a total of fifteen teachers in Negro schools, five were native whites; in Barnwell County the only Negro school in existence was one conducted by a native white woman; in 1867, in the eight-county area termed the department of western South Carolina, fifteen of the twenty-six teachers in the area were white Southerners.[37]

Whites were thus neither one thing nor the other entirely in their attitudes toward Negro schooling. Many of them opposed it, while at the same time many gave it their encouragement. One generalization seems valid, however. After 1867 white opposition to schools supported and taught by Northerners grew decidedly more pronounced, a development stemming largely out of the political feeling aroused in the state by the Radical Reconstruction program of that year and the establishment of a new state government, controlled by Radical supporters, in 1868. Whites came increasingly to believe that Northern teachers were using their classrooms less to educate than to indoctrinate, less to instruct than to propagandize in behalf of the Republican party. Superintendent Tomlinson, commenting upon this phenomenon, observed: "The principal reason assigned in justification of this wish to get rid of Northern teachers is that Politics is taught in our Schools."[38] White spokesmen based their opposition on various grounds. Northern teachers, some of them com-

36. Columbia *Daily Phoenix*, June 25, 1868.
37. *Keowee Courier*, April 22, 1870; Charleston *Courier*, January 18, 1867; Yorkville *Inquirer*, July 26, 1866; Laurensville *Herald*, August 5, 1867; Charleston *Daily News*, June 26, 1867; William Nerland to Scott, April 30, 1867, Bureau Records, S. C., Vol. 126; J. D. Greene to Scott, October 30, 1866; *ibid.*, Vol. 132; Samuel Place to Scott, September 22, 1866, *ibid.*, Box 518.
38. Scott to Howard, August 14, 1868, Bureau Records, S. C., Vol. 13.

plained, too often used the classrooms to belittle the South, to advocate social equality, and to instill in the freedmen ideas that made for ill feeling between the races.[39] Others objected to the Fourth-of-July ceremonies at the schools which frequently included tributes to men who had become anathema to the South. A typical example was one offered by the children to John Brown:[40]

> Who talks of deeds of high renown?
>   I sing the valiant martyr Brown.
> I love the Doctor of the West,
>   May his pure soul in quiet rest.
> Let Nations weep the martyr's death,
>   Let children lisp with early breath,
> The name of Brown, above all men,
>   Who e'er have lived in mortal ken.

In this air of mounting white opposition in the state and spreading apathy in the North about Negro education, the Bureau's superintendent could not but feel a deep pessimism as he brought the agency's educational endeavor to a close in 1870. Noting that the cause of education for the freedmen was but in its infancy, he went on: "Hereafter, it must devolve upon the state authorities. While I have confidence in the intentions of the State Superintendent to forward the work . . . , I am fully aware of the futility of his exertions when measured against the ignorance and stupidity of the county school officials and the comparative indifference of our Legislature, to this cause. I therefore close my connection with this work with gloomy forebodings."[41]

39. J. R. Edie to Howard, October 19, 1868, Bureau Records, S. C., Vol. 13; William Stone to J. R. Edie, June 1, 1868, *ibid.*, Box 521; Tomlinson to Scott, July 1, 1867, Bureau Records, Box 1098.

40. Sumter *Watchman,* July 18, 1866.

41. E. L. Deane to Howard, July 15, 1870, Bureau Records, Box 1098. Deane's pessimism was confirmed by the course of events. The authorities on Reconstruction in the state declare that the superintendent of education for the next six years was merely an "official clerk" whose duties consisted principally of "passing on to careless commissioners what portion of the school funds the administrators and legislators did not divert to improper uses." Simkins and Woody, *South Carolina During Reconstruction,* pp. 437-38. In 1902 a national authority wrote: "The legislature [of South Carolina] . . . was either ignorant, indifferent, or culpably insincere in its dealings with the public school interest through the entire period of reconstruction." A. D. Mayo, *The Work of Certain Northern Churches in the*

This note of ending contrasted very strikingly with that voiced in the beginning in 1865. It was, unhappily, a note more nearly in tune with the reality than had been the dreams and hopes of five years before. To be sure, a substantial effort had been made during the five-year period. Over half a million dollars had been spent on the cause of Negro education, about one-fourth of which had come from the Bureau and the rest from private groups and individuals. Perhaps twenty to thirty thousand Negro children had gained some instruction in the schools, some of them getting enough education to go forth as teachers of other freedmen. And the whole effort, at least, had held up a noble vision— that of a people, by education, raising themselves up to become worthy of the challenge and opportunity which lay before them. Yet so much—so very much—had been left undone. Three-fourths of the Negro children of school age had been entirely unreached by the educational effort. Nor is it wholly certain that those who had studied in the schools were basically any better equipped to fashion their destiny in a world of freedom, since the curriculum was so often unrealistic in how it sought to answer the needs of a people just arising from bondage. Finally, the fervent emotionalism which had motivated the Northern response in the beginning proved a fragile thing, for as it burned itself out it helped to kill the momentum of the whole movement. The history of Negro education in South Carolina after 1870 is an unhappy testament to this fact.

A conclusion of the Bureau's national superintendent of education in 1870 about the South as a whole could apply with particular relevance to South Carolina:

> The masses of these freedmen are still ignorant. Educational associations unaided by Government will largely fall off. The States south, as a whole, awake but slowly to the instruction of their lower classes. No one of them is fully prepared . . . to sustain these schools; the colored people yet in poverty and unacquainted with school institutions, even the most elementary; opposition latent, indeed, but still existing. Who will lead on these dependent multitudes? Who will guide this mighty current of awakened thought and aspiration? With sorrow we anticipate . . . the closing

Education of the Freedmen, 1861-1900, Report of the Commissioner of Education, 1902 (Washington, 1903), I, 1026.

of hundreds of these school buildings, and sending thousands of children . . . to the streets, or what is far worse, to squalid houses, to grow up, not as props and pillars of society, but its pests. Even what has been done, and well done, will we fear, prove but half done if unfinished.[42]

Time alone would prove the prophetic accuracy of such forebodings.

42. Report of the Secretary of War, *House Executive Document*, 41 Cong., 3 Sess., no. 1 (serial 1446), pp. 322-23.

In its concern for the general welfare of the freedmen, the Bureau devoted its main attention to the questions of relief, land, labor, and education, but it did not neglect other matters which, though smaller in scope, were nevertheless relevant to the total meaning of freedom. These miscellaneous concerns, though peripheral in importance, still had a bearing upon the question of how free the former bondsmen were to become. One of these matters was that concerning the legal rights of the freedmen. By war and by law they were no longer slaves in 1865, but neither, as yet, were they clothed with the guarantees of citizenship. And until the adoption of the Fourteenth Amendment, and the ratification of the new state constitution in South Carolina in 1868, their legal status remained unsure and unclear. Meantime, the Bureau was theoretically responsible for defining and protecting their legal rights; in practice its jurisdiction was repeatedly circumscribed by action of the state authorities and Federal military commanders. The result was conflict and confusion, described by an observer in 1866 as, "Wheels within wheels, Blackstone hemmed in with bayonets, and clients and counsels sadly bewildered."[1]

Following the surrender of Southern armies, the governor of the state undertook to continue the wartime administration, but soon found the move countermanded and himself arrested by Union military order. To maintain peace and dispense justice, the Federal commander stationed garrisons in various counties, established military courts, and directed that serious crimes were to be tried before military commissions while misdemeanors were to be handled by provost courts. The latter, to consist normally of one officer and two "loyal citizens," were to hear cases in which the maximum punishment amounted to a fine of one hundred dollars or two months' imprisonment.[2] Meanwhile,

1. Charleston *Courier*, March 22, 1866.
2. *Ibid.*, July 6, 1865.

Rufus Saxton was developing the organization of the Bureau in the state and, under instructions from General Howard, directing his subordinates to assume jurisdiction over all cases between Negroes and whites where civil courts either did not exist or, if existing, refused to admit Negro testimony.[3] From the very beginning, thus, a conflict in jurisdiction developed between the Bureau and the military authorities.

As the months passed the conflict grew and the situation became more confused, in part because of the peculiar status of those army officers who were also Bureau officials. In some respects they were subject to military authority, in others to that of the Bureau. When the two authorities disagreed and issued conflicting orders, as happened with increasing frequency, the officer found himself in a quandary over which course to take— and often it was the innocent freedman who suffered from the resulting confusion. The situation was thrown into further disarray in the summer of 1865 when, under the presidential reconstruction policy, a provisional government was created and the new governor, B. F. Perry, sought to revive a system of state courts with jurisdiction over all cases, including those involving freedmen. In an effort to clarify the question Perry met with Federal military commanders in September. The result was an agreement that, in the future, cases affecting whites would be heard by civil tribunals while those involving freedmen would be handled by provost courts until such time as state law recognized the admissibility of Negro testimony. When Howard learned of the arrangement he protested that it usurped the Bureau's authority concerning the Negro's legal rights, but to no avail.[4]

Certainly, though, the need for some such agreement, and for immediate action, was real and even urgent. From all over the state came reports in the summer and fall which told of violence against the Negro and flagrant abuse of his rights as a free man. Saxton, for example, said that he had "every reason to believe" an agent who had reported finding several bodies of murdered Negroes through the woods in his district near Beaufort.[5] In an-

3. General Order #3, June 26, 1865, Bureau Records, S. C., Box 496.
4. Charleston *Courier*, September 5, 1865; B. F. Perry, *Reminiscences of Public Men* (Greenville, 1889), pp. 270-71.
5. Saxton to Howard, June 4, 1865, Bureau Records, S. C., Box 487.

other case an agent related that in his area the whites had organized a band of regulators to enforce among the Negroes a pass-system similar to that used during slavery.[6] In still a different section a Bureau officer, after compiling a long list of crimes against Negroes, wrote: "If the Black Man is free & has common rights before the law, why should he not be treated as such? The present course pursued towards him is very disgraceful & calls aloud for justice."[7] Nor were the outrages always by local whites. In a number of instances they were by Federal troops who sometimes vented their racial prejudice as abusively as Southern whites. Sidney Andrews, for example, reported cases in which Northern soldiers used the lash upon freedmen, and a local paper described an episode in which some of them wantonly attacked Negroes and then set fire to one of their schoolhouses.[8]

Many of the reported outrages were probably overdrawn, and some were clearly based on hearsay evidence. Yet they show clearly enough that the freedom of the Negro in theory was one thing, and the security of his legal rights quite another. Thus, the need for military action was imperative. Throughout 1865 provost courts were thronged with freedmen seeking redress of their grievances, large and small. Meantime, the state legislature, despite the agreement between Governor Perry and the military commander, undertook to provide a new definition of the legal status of the Negro and to give jurisdiction over him to state courts. Among other things, this "black code" allowed freedmen to own property, to sue and be sued, and to testify in cases in which they alone were involved; on the other hand, it declared their testimony inadmissible in cases involving white litigants and it prescribed heavier penalties for Negroes than for whites in certain kinds of crimes.[9] But the Federal commander soon declared the code invalid and directed the provost courts to continue their jurisdiction over cases involving freed-

6. J. C. Beecher to Saxton, October 7, 1865, Bureau Records, S. C., Box 470.

7. F. M. Mantell to Saxton, undated, Bureau Records, S. C., Box 472.

8. Sidney Andrews, *The South Since the War* (Boston, 1866), p. 206; *Keowee Courier*, April 14, 1866. See also E. A. Kozlay to Saxton, October 10, 1865, Bureau Records, S. C., Box 470, and C. S. Brown to C. H. Howard, October 23, 1865, *ibid.*, Box 487.

9. Francis B. Simkins and Robert H. Woody, *South Carolina During Reconstruction* (Chapel Hill, 1932), pp. 48-51.

men. On occasion he also went a step further, once by ordering the arrest of several prominent citizens of Edgefield on charges of complicity in the murder of a freedman, and again by threatening to evacuate the Negroes of three counties at the whites' expense unless the Negroes there were treated more humanely.[10]

Throughout it all the Bureau found itself virtually powerless, either to define or to protect the legal rights of the freedmen. Agents, of course, could and did use their office to settle trivial disputes among Negroes, or between Negro and white. But in more serious matters they could only inform the nearest military commander or submit requests that troops be detached for their use in arresting whites charged with crimes against freedmen—requests that more often than not appear to have been ignored or denied. Nor was this all. Bureau officials, as well as freedmen, often complained that the provost courts were exhibiting considerable racial prejudice in the justice they dispensed. A group of freedmen in Columbia, for example, protested that the provost courts there imposed heavier penalties on Negroes than on whites for the same crime, and required Negro litigants, unlike the whites, to post bond before they were allowed to institute a case. Such discrimination, they declared, led them to feel that they had been more secure under slavery than under freedom. They had gained nothing, they added, by having firearms "substituted for the lash—& in having a freedman's life valued by a court as worth no more than $5."[11] Assistant Commissioner Scott wrote at the close of 1866 that in some instances Negroes had walked a hundred miles or more to his headquarters to secure justice, because in many regions they feared Federal troops "as much as they do their former masters."[12]

Concerned over the status of affairs in South Carolina, Commissioner Howard in the summer of 1866 persuaded the Secretary of War to allow Scott to assume command of the troops in the state, subject only to the general authority of the departmental

10. General Order #1, January 1, 1866, Bureau Records, S. C., Vol. 26; Charleston *Daily News*, December 7, 1866.

11. Petition of freedmen to Scott, undated, Bureau Records, S. C., Box 475. Typical examples of provost court cases and decisions can be found in Bureau Records, S. C., Vols. 94, 127, 211, and 239.

12. Annual Report of Scott, November 1, 1866, Bureau Records, Box 778. See also G. W. Gile to Scott, July 30, 1866, Bureau Records, S. C., Box 475, and W. J. Whipper to Scott, November 21, 1866, *ibid.*, Box 476.

commander. The Commissioner hoped that this step, in addition to lessening the Bureau–military friction, would also enable the Bureau to play a more positive role in securing justice for the Negro.[13] A short time later, basing his action upon the provisions of the Second Freedmen's Bureau Bill of July, he went a step further and authorized the creation of Bureau courts wherever state law discriminated against freedmen. These courts, he specified, were to consist of three members and were to exercise jurisdiction over all civil cases pertaining to Negroes where the sum involved was not more than $300.[14] But neither of Howard's schemes proved successful. In the case of the first, Scott soon complained that his expanded military authority was more apparent than real, since the commanding general of the department reserved to himself "the right of ordering the movement of troops, and the establishment of posts and garrisons."[15] In the case of the second, President Johnson disapproved the order authorizing the establishment of Bureau courts, partly because he questioned its constitutional validity, and partly because the decision by the Supreme Court in the Milligan Case earlier in the year seemed clearly to prohibit such interference with the judicial system of a state. Consequently, Howard was compelled to tell Scott and other assistant commissioners to use their own discretion in trying to insure justice for the freedmen.[16]

The practical outcome in South Carolina was that the Bureau's role in securing the legal rights of the Negro continued to be limited to such minor disputes as individual agents could settle, while all matters of consequence remained under the jurisdiction of provost courts. Then in October, 1866, the entire picture changed when the legislature, by formal action, opened the

13. Annual Report of Scott, November 1, 1866, Bureau Records, Box 778.
14. Howard to Scott, September 19, 1866, Bureau Records, S. C., Box 502.
15. Annual Report of Scott, November 1, 1866, Bureau Records, Box 778.
16. George R. Bentley, A History of the Freedmen's Bureau (Philadelphia, 1955), pp. 162-68. Howard made an unsuccessful effort early in 1867 to get before the courts a test case involving the section of the bill creating the Bureau which had authorized the establishment of Bureau courts. He asked Scott if it were possible to "get a judge of a U. S. Court, to take from a Military Commission . . . a case of 'Habeas Corpus' and carry it up to the Supreme Court," but Scott was unable to find a suitable case. Howard to Scott, January 30, 1867, and Scott's reply, February 5, 1867, Bureau Records, S. C., Box 479.

courts of the state to Negroes on a basis of equality and declared their testimony to be legally admissible in all litigation. Thereupon, the departmental commander ordered the disestablishment of provost courts throughout the state, save for two or three areas where they were to continue, and directed that, henceforth, military officials should turn over to state courts all cases involving freedmen.[17] From this point on, the question of the Negro's legal rights became and remained mainly one for civilian tribunals to determine, though until the establishment of the new state regime in 1868, military authorities continued on occasion to intervene in cases where local judges failed to administer justice fairly between the races.

Thus, the Bureau was eliminated from even its nominal role in the matter. Nevertheless, Assistant Commissioner Scott instructed his subordinates to inform him of any cases of legal irregularities involving the rights of the freedmen, hoping that he might use the influence of his position to secure for them impartial justice. And, on occasion, he authorized agents to employ legal assistance for the defense of Negroes.[18] From time to time his agents did report instances of judicial discrimination against the Negroes, though others reported favorably upon the justice of local judges. One, for example, wrote that in his area the Negro was treated with entire fairness—"his evidence is accepted, his suits are entertained, his complaints heard."[19] Another offered a similar appraisal for his district and noted that, in addition, white lawyers had agreed to represent Negro clients, even against whites.[20] J. W. De Forest declared that, of a total of fifty or sixty magistrates in his three-county region, he had found only one unfit for office because of racial prejudice. "New York City," he added, "would be fortunate if it could have justice

17. Charleston *Daily News*, October 6, 1866.

18. Scott to A. E. Niles, February 6, 1867, Bureau Records, S. C., Vol. 221.

19. J. W. De Forest to Scott, October 31, 1866, Bureau Records, S. C., Box 526. For typical expressions of opposite points of view, see: George Gile to Scott, August 31, 1866, *ibid.*, Vol. 175; W. H. Stone to Scott, October 20, 1866, *ibid.*, Vol. 87; E. R. Chase to Scott, October 17, 1866, *ibid.*, Vol. 90.

20. George Gile to Scott, August 31, 1866, Bureau Records, S. C., Vol. 175.

dealt out to it as honestly and as fairly as it was dealt out by the plain, homespun farmers. . . ."[21]

Because its authority never equalled its concern, the Bureau was unable to play a role of any great consequence in defining and then securing the legal rights of the freedmen in the state. Caught between military force and state authority, it found itself all but excluded from a question of direct bearing upon the Negro's freedom. Nevertheless, it did manage to make some contribution, even if small, to the story. It seems reasonable to assume that, by its very presence and its known concern for the rights of the freedmen, it helped to secure for them a legal equality from local officials which otherwise may have been longer deferred. Moreover, agents and officers, by mediating thousands of small quarrels and petty disputes, doubtless impressed upon many freedmen the rule of having their grievances redressed by appeal to an impartial authority instead of resorting to personal revenge. Thereby, they helped to define one of freedom's actualities for the former slaves.

Another concern of the Bureau, in its regard for the whole well-being of the freedmen, was the regularizing of their marriage status, a question which was both complex and delicate. In the first place slave marriages had not enjoyed the sanctity of normal legal standing, and in the second, many Negro slaves, through forced separation or for other reasons, had lived successively with more than one marital partner. Sometimes a man who was sold from one owner to another may have had three or more wives in succession and fathered children by all three, while his previous wives, meantime, may have remarried and borne children by the new husband. With the coming of freedom considerable confusion inevitably developed over the question of legal and moral responsibility among husbands and wives.

Early in his administration Assistant Commissioner Saxton asked Mansfield French, a minister of wide experience with the Sea Island Experiment during the war, to undertake the regularizing of marriage relations among the freedmen. In August of 1865 French issued a circular designed to clear up much of

21. John W. De Forest, *A Union Officer in the Reconstruction* (New Haven, 1948), p. 31.

the uncertainty surrounding the matter.[22] By its terms of definition, the only legally married freedmen were to be those who
were living together as man and wife at the time of emancipation,
or whose marriage had been properly solemnized since. All
those who had been married during slavery with nothing more
formal than the master's consent were directed to secure from
some minister of a recognized church or some civil magistrate a
marriage certificate; unless they did so, the circular declared,
they would not be allowed to continue to live together. Normally, husbands and wives separated from each other during slavery
could reunite as marital partners provided that they could secure
a statement attesting to their marriage from some church or
benevolent society. If either partner of a slave marriage could
present evidence of separation from the spouse for at least three
years and further evidence that the spouse had married again
or had died, then that partner was free to engage in a new
marriage.

Not all cases could be this simply adjusted. If a man, twice
married during slavery but living alone in 1865, should find
himself with both wives restored, one with children by him and
one without, he must choose the former. Apparently, if neither
wife had children the man was free to take either. Likewise, if a
childless woman should be claimed by two former husbands, she
could choose either. Provision was even made whereby a man
currently married could take an earlier wife, provided that she
had borne children by him, that she had no other known husband, and that the second wife gave her consent. In any case,
if the man adamantly refused to remarry an earlier mate by
whom he had fathered children, he must still assume their legal
support; and if the wife refused to renew her ties with a former
husband, he could secure release of all obligations to her by
getting a divorce, which every recognized church or benevolent
society was authorized to grant, either for moral cause or for
prudential reasons growing out of the confusion of slave re-
lationships. Whenever a wife won a separation on grounds of

22. Mansfield French, *Address to Masters and Freedmen* (Macon, 1865);
the marriage regulations can also be found in *House Executive Document*,
39 Cong., 1 Sess., no. 70 (serial 1238), pp. 108-11. For the role of French
in the Sea Island Experiment, see Willie Lee Rose, *Rehearsal for Reconstruction: The Port Royal Experiment* (Indianapolis, 1964), *passim*.

adultery, one-half of the husband's personal property and all of the household goods were to go to her.[23]

Couples who married or remarried under the new arrangement were issued a standard marriage certificate.[24] Bordered all around with passages such as "What therefore God hath joined together let not man put asunder," it read simply:

CERTIFICATE OF MARRIAGE

This CERTIFIES that Mary Green of Ladies Island and Richard Burke of the same island have this day been joined together as husband and wife, after God's holy ordinance of MARRIAGE, until separated by death.

DATED at Beaufort, S. C., January 27, 1866.

T. Peck, OFFICIATING MINISTER

It is impossible to say how many marriages among the freedmen were regularized by terms of the circular, and how many by the common sense of the Negroes themselves in responding to the new circumstances. But in any case, the whole question was ultimately given formal regularity by laws of the state legislature, containing basically the same provisions as the circular of French.[25] Freedmen themselves, during 1865 and 1866, enthusiastically responded to the new dispensation, eager to assume this further manifestation of their status as free men and women. One result was, as the formalization process required, that they added a surname, often that of their former owners, to the lone Christian name by which most had been known as slaves. Another result was that many, even those who had lived together as husband and wife for many years, experienced a new meaningfulness and felt a new dignity as they formally took the marriage vows. One observer, commenting upon a wedding among the freedmen, described it as "so interesting and so hallowed, that it really seemed that the angels . . . were hovering on joyous wings over the scene."[26] Still another result was the stimulus given to

23. General Order #8, August 11, 1865, Bureau Records, S. C., Box 496.
24. This particular copy is in Box 511, Bureau Records, S. C.
25. For various aspects of the question, see Circular Letter from Howard, March 2, 1866, Bureau Records, S. C., Box 476; Mansfield French to Scott, November 6, 1866, *ibid.*, Box 474; Simkins and Woody, *South Carolina During Reconstruction*, pp. 48-52; Charleston *Courier*, March 9, 1866.
26. Mansfield French to Scott, November 6, 1866, Bureau Records,

the formation of the Negro family, separate and distinct from the families of other Negroes; and in this respect, according to several observers, free Negroes as distinguished from freed, and mulattoes as distinguished from blacks, early began to cultivate a feeling of exclusiveness within their own society. In Greenville, wrote John W. De Forest, "there was a deep and increasing jealousy between the blacks and mulattoes. To some extent they formed distinct cliques of society and crystallized into separate churches."[27] Still a fourth result of the regularization of marriage was the tendency for the man to become the undisputed head of the household. Laura M. Towne wrote that this right "to have their own way in their families and rule their wives" was regarded as "an inestimable privilege."[28]

Another endeavor of the Bureau in its concern for the whole well-being of the freedmen had to do with the cause of temperance among them. General Howard, who held an almost passionate aversion to drinking, was eager to have the Bureau use its influence among the Negroes to promote the cause of abstinence. He hoped to enlist the co-operation of the National Sons of Temperance in the crusade, but finding that its leaders "retain their old bigotry" through insisting upon segregated chapters, he advised his subordinates to encourage the freedmen to form their own organizations under the name of the Lincoln Temperance Society.[29] How strongly Howard felt on the general matter is revealed by a letter he wrote Assistant Commissioner Scott on one occasion. Discovering that many freedmen at Beaufort were patronizing "a rum hole in their midst," he sternly declared: "I had thought of aiding an institution for the education of teachers in this vicinity, but if the colored people are determined to support rum shops at Beaufort, I will not appropriate one cent of the public money for such an institution at that place."[30]

To further the goals under Howard's program, Scott urged

S. C., Box 474; Elizabeth H. Botume, *First Days Among the Contrabands* (Boston, 1893), p. 160.

27. De Forest, *A Union Officer*, p. 124. See also *The Nation*, I (August 10, 1865), 173, (December 21, 1865), 779; Botume, *First Days Among the Contrabands*, pp. 120-121; 132-33.

28. Rupert S. Holland (ed.), *Letters and Diary of Laura M. Towne* (Cambridge, 1912), p. 184.

29. Howard to Scott, May 15, 1867, Bureau Records, S. C., Box 479.

30. Howard to Scott, May 4, 1867, Bureau Records, S. C., Box 479.

his agents throughout the state to promote temperance leagues among the freedmen and sent them a supply of printed temperance pledges to be used.[31] Whether the campaign produced any deep or lasting effect among the Negroes is questionable. Some agents reported that freedmen were responding to the campaign enthusiastically, others that they were indifferent towards the whole matter. John W. De Forest, for example, though observing that the freedmen "were unquestionably less addicted to ardent spirits than the Southern whites," wrote: "I soon discovered that if I wanted to raise a 'snicker' . . . I had only to exhibit one of . . . [the temperance pledges] and explain its purpose. . . . I never got a signature; nothing but snickers and guffaws—irrepressible anti-temperance laughter."[32] But whether successful or not, the endeavor reveals another dimension of the Bureau's concern for the whole well-being of the freedmen.

At the same time that the agency was trying to discourage drinking among the freedmen, it was also seeking to encourage habits of thrift by urging them to deposit their money in the Freedman's Bank. Chartered by Congress in March of 1865 as the Freedman's Savings and Trust Company, the institution was the outgrowth of wartime efforts by various Union commanders to establish banks in their departments for Negro soldiers. Created for the exclusive use of Negroes, the Bank was required to invest at least two-thirds of its deposits in government securities, allowed to pay a maximum interest rate of seven per cent, and authorized to use any surplus funds for the promotion of the cause of Negro education.[33]

Legally the Bureau and the Bank were not related, but in fact the relationship between them was extremely close. General Howard, though declining an offered position with the institutions, strongly endorsed the Bank in a statement which was printed in every depositor's passbook, and urged his subordinates to give the institution their energetic support.[34] J. W. Alvord, the Bureau's superintendent of education, served as corresponding

31. Scott to all agents, August 15, 1867, Bureau Records, S. C., Box 510; E. W. Everson to Mansfield French, June 6, 1867, *ibid.*, Vol. 235.

32. De Forest, *A Union Officer*, p. 103.

33. Walter L. Fleming, *The Freedmen's Savings Bank: A Chapter in the Economic History of the Negro Race* (Chapel Hill, 1927), pp. 19-22, 30-34.

34. *Ibid.*, pp. 44-46.

secretary and then as president of the Bank; and in South Carolina a number of Bureau officials, including Rufus Saxton, served
in some official capacity with it there. Moreover, the Bureau
often provided rent-free office space to the Bank in various cities,
and in some instances assistant commissioners gave Bureau positions to Bank personnel.[35] Thus, it is not surprising that freedmen should have regarded the Bank as a branch of the Bureau.

With its national charter which implied its endorsement by
the Federal government and the strong support given by the
Bureau, the Bank attracted a widespread response from the
freedmen, ultimately operating over thirty branches throughout
the South, in New York, Pennsylvania, and the District of Columbia. Total deposits grew from $300,000 in 1866 to $57,000,000
in 1874.[36] In South Carolina the first branch was opened at
Beaufort in October, 1865, and a second at Charleston a short
time later. Both branches, in light of the poverty of the former
slaves, proved surprisingly successful. During 1866, according to
General Scott, freedmen in the state deposited nearly $100,000.[37]
In the following year the Charleston *Courier* reported that the
branch in that city, whose depositors numbered nearly nineteen
hundred, was averaging about $20,000 a month in receipts.[38]

Much of the early success of the Bank, of course, can be explained by its close association with the Bureau, since for a time
"nearly every bank official wore the uniform of the United States;
the Bureau offices and the branch banks were often in the same
rooms; and the missionaries and agents of the Bureau regularly
solicited deposits."[39] No less important, however, was the per-
suasive and skillful advertising of the Bank itself. Especially
effective was the passbook for depositors, containing illustrations,
quotations, and poems lauding the principle of thrift.[40] The out-

35. Howard to U. S. Littlefield, July 10, 1865, Bureau Records, S. C.,
Box 473; Saxton to J. A. Bogart, August 7, 1865, *ibid.*, Vol. 9; J. W. Alvord
to Scott, March 19, 1866, *ibid.*, Box 476; Circular Letter from Howard, May
7, 1867, *ibid.*, Box 479; Fleming, *Freedmen's Savings Bank*, pp. 32-39.

36. Fleming, *Freedmen's Savings Bank*, pp. 50-51. See also *The Nation*,
I (December 21, 1865), 779.

37. Annual Report of Scott, November 1, 1866, Bureau Records, S. C.,
Vol. 11. See also Annual Report of Saxton, December 6, 1865, Bureau
Records, Box 732.

38. July 18, 1867.

39. Fleming, *Freedmen's Savings Bank*, p. 37.

40. A copy of the passbook from which the illustrations were chosen is
among the Scott Papers.

side cover carried a picture of the Washington office, with the notation in bold letters that it was opposite the "TREASURY," obviously encouraging the belief that the Bank had the financial backing of the Federal government. Inside the passbook were various statements designed to show that the institution was endorsed by a number of prominent figures, including one that the Bank had received "the commendation and countenance of ABRAHAM LINCOLN," whose approval of the charter constituted one of "the last official acts of the martyred President."

Poetry and parables were also used to extol the virtues of thrift. One poem read in part:

'Tis little by little an ant gets her store
    Every little we add to the little makes more;
Step by step we walk miles, and we sew stitch by stitch
    Word by word we read books, cent by cent we grow rich.

One of the parables used told of a man who, upon discovering that he spent $52 a year on tobacco and only $42 for bread, decided to quit smoking; in ten years his savings, at the prevailing rate of interest, would amount to $669.52. The final entry on the inside back cover read:

Bank of Happiness—THE SAVINGS BANK
Bank of Misery—THE WHISKY SHOP
Bank of Idleness—THE LOTTERY SHOP

With the help of the Bureau, the Bank continued to expand its operations and, in all probability, helped to instill in many freedmen the lesson of thrift and saving. But the good it accomplished was more than offset by its sudden collapse in 1874, caused partly by the depression of the previous year, but mainly from fraud and mismanagement by its directors.[41] Negroes who had responded in good faith to the savings campaign of the Bureau and the Bank now found all their investments irrecoverably lost. And so an endeavor so praiseworthy in its purpose ended at length in disaster for a large number.

Still another area in which the Bureau strove to promote the well-being of the freedmen was that pertaining to pensions, bounties, and other payments that were due Negro soldiers and

41. For a discussion of the reasons behind the failure, see Fleming, *Freedmen's Savings Bank*, Chap. V.

their families. Volunteer soldiers of the Union Army, upon being honorably discharged, were entitled to a certain bounty beyond their regular pay; in the event of their death in service, the bounty went to their families. Many were also entitled to other payments such as shares of prize money. But often, Negro soldiers or their widows were defrauded by unscrupulous lawyers or dishonest claims agents.

To minimize the possibility of such fraud, General Howard, early in the Bureau's history, instructed officers and agents to render all possible assistance to freedmen in filing claims for various funds to which they were entitled. In the following year he organized a claims division within the Bureau, and shortly thereafter Congress made it the sole agent for paying the claims of Negro soldiers and sailors. To further protect the freedmen the Commissioner instructed his subordinates to deduct from the claims payment any legal fee owed to a lawyer or agent, pay it to him, and then personally deliver the remainder to the Negro, cautioning him not to pay any further fees to any agent.[42] At length the new arrangement was so efficient that Howard, with pardonable pride, could write, "The machinery for paying these bounties is now so perfect that payment is made without loss to the claimants."[43] All told, between 1867 and 1872, the Bureau handled claims of freedmen amounting to over nine million dollars.[44] Thereby, it enabled thousands of Negro veterans and their families to secure, honestly and efficiently, the claims which justly belonged to them.

None of these miscellaneous concerns of the Bureau, nor all of them together, were of critical bearing upon the future of the Negro. Certainly, they did not approach in importance the major questions like relief, land, labor, and education. Yet however indirectly, they did affect the total dimensions of freedom for the former slaves; to the extent that the Bureau succeeded in

42. Bentley, *Freedmen's Bureau*, p. 148. See also Circular #12, July 14, 1865, from Howard's office, Bureau Records, S. C., Box 473; and O. O. Howard, *Autobiography of Oliver Otis Howard* (New York, 1907), II, 293-94.

43. Bentley, *Freedmen's Bureau*, p. 148.

44. Report of the Secretary of War, *House Executive Document*, 42 Cong., 2 Sess., no. 1 (serial 1503), pp. 451-52.

these varied endeavors, those dimensions were enlarged and made more meaningful.[45]

45. One final indirect aid given by Bureau officials in the state should be mentioned briefly. In mid-1867 Scott requested of all subordinates a contribution to be given to Howard College, in order to give needed financial help and also to make a gesture of affection towards Howard himself. In all, a total of at least $450—and possibly more, since the records are not clear—was given. Scott to all agents, August 19, 1867, Bureau Records, S. C., Vol. 12; Howard to Scott, October 8, 1867, *ibid.*, Box 536.

Unlike later generations of their kinsmen, whites in South Carolina in 1865 saw little romance among the charred embers of the Confederacy. To most, the Lost Cause was not so much a drama as a tale of woe and anguish. Nor was the grim aftermath of war made more pleasant by the presence in force of the conqueror—troops, teachers, Treasury agents, and Bureau officials from the North spreading out over the state. As time passed, native whites came to feel and express an increasing resentment towards what they viewed as an effort by Northerners to refashion the pattern of Southern life, especially where the question of race relations was involved. And since it was this very question that lay at the heart of the Bureau's work, that agency became an object of especial disdain.

Both then and later, white spokesmen developed a stereotyped view of the Bureau, its work and its personnel, that would become in time a part of the folklore about the dark excesses of Reconstruction. One white South Carolinian, for example, could write in 1907, with relative mildness, that the agency, though praiseworthy in its intentions, "did much more harm than good"; it had encouraged Negroes by free rations to become "idlers and vagrants" and, by its interference, had damaged "the mutual kindly regard" which had formerly existed between the two races.[1] Another native, writing shortly after Reconstruction had ended, was much harsher in describing the Bureau as a swindling machine "in the hands of sharpers" which had spread "its filthy meshes all over the State." He added: "These man-traps furnished appropriate schooling for that rapacious crew who afterwards revelled in the treasury of the State."[2]

Although white opposition towards the Bureau would not assumed stereotyped proportions until later years, it began al-

1. Edward L. Wells, *Hampton and Reconstruction* (Columbia, 1907), p. 75.
2. John A. Leland, *A Voice from South Carolina: Twelve Chapters Before Hampton, Two Chapters After Hampton* (Charleston, 1879), p. 34.

most at once as a part of the general anti-Northern resentment that prevailed in many native white quarters. Sidney Andrews, as he toured the state in the fall of 1865, often encountered a strong dislike for "Yankees," occasionally so pronounced that innkeepers refused to rent him a room.[3] When General Daniel Sickles, commanding officer in the state, enrolled his daughter in a private school in Charleston, many citizens sharply criticized the school's director for accepting her, and at least one mother withdrew her child from the institution in protest.[4] One white spokesman, expressing what must have been a common sentiment, spoke caustically of the "bullying insolence and inflated arrogance of the Yankees" and, then, even more scornfully, of his fellow whites who stooped to associating with Northerners. Such *"fawning toadyism* and *truckling flunkeyism of our own people,"* he fumed, *". . . are thoroughly and insupportably contemptible."*[5] An officer told of a white planter who, seeking rations for his freed workers, came to Bureau headquarters and then, his mission complete, lingered to talk for a while. As he was leaving, he inquired where the officer lived; upon being told and invited to make a social call, the planter replied with some heat, "I will do so; I want to see you somewhere outside this d—d bureau."[6] The perceptive John W. De Forest wryly observed about his status: "It must be remembered that to my native infamy as a Yankee I added the turpitude of being a United States military officer and the misdemeanor of being a sub-assistant commissioner of the Freedmen's Bureau."[7]

In such a climate of white hostility towards Northerners individually and collectively, the Bureau inevitably became a target of criticism and attack. Even had its record been what it was not, one of near-perfection, it seems clear that it still would have aroused white hostility. Being human and thus fallible, it made its full share of mistakes, thereby affording its critics additional cause to complain of its presence. Certainly some of its leaders

3. Sidney Andrews, *The South Since the War* (Boston, 1866), p. 16.
4. Elizabeth W. Pringle, *Chronicles of Chicora Wood* (Boston, 1940), pp. 325-26.
5. Sumter *Watchman*, June 13, 1866.
6. *Report of the Joint Committee on Reconstruction at the First Session, Thirty-Ninth Congress* (Washington, 1866), p. 234.
7. John W. De Forest, *A Union Officer in the Reconstruction* (New Haven, 1948), p. 187.

were tactless in reminding white Carolinians, quite unnecessarily, that they had lost the war and must adapt themselves to the changed order of things. General Saxton, for example, was hardly a model of discretion when, in his very first circular as assistant commissioner, he implied a Northern monopoly on the services of God during the war by admonishing "the late masters" to "heed the teachings of the great struggle" and "accept the result as the verdict of the Almighty against human slavery."[8]

But more important than the temperament of individual Bureau officers in shaping white attitudes were the major actions taken by the Bureau in performing its work. Its role in handling captured and abandoned lands, for example, drew the wrath of white spokesmen, one of whom bitterly asked: "Why should we be wanderers—homeless & houseless, many of us dependent upon Charity, and our homes given to negroes, who surely have done no more for the U. S. Government than we . . . ?"[9] The Charleston *Courier* also felt deeply aggrieved by the Bureau's work in the matter of land distribution. Terming the presence of the agency "anomalous and unnecessary" and its work as one that promoted social chaos, the editorial went on to declare: "Those are the real enemies of the freedmen who seek to instill in them that they can either be prosperous or progressive, except by the ordinary conditions of frugality, sobriety, and honest, consistent toil."[10] With some exaggeration, Saxton once wrote that "the late rebels hate and slander us. They are profoundly impressed with the belief . . . that a 'black man has no rights which a white man is bound to respect.' They see in this bureau a great stumbling block in the way of their schemes to overthrow the policy of the government and make the freedman a slave in everything but name."[11]

In actuality, as discussed in an earlier chapter, by the close of 1865 the Bureau, under presidential order, was proceeding steadily to restore confiscated property to its original owners. Nevertheless, freedmen continued to hope and somehow to believe that the land was yet to be divided among them. And as this hope lingered white spokesmen viewed it, not as an expression of a people's longing, but as an indication that Northern-

8. Circular #1, June 10, 1865, Bureau Records, S. C., Box 496.
9. Lillian Kibler, *Benjamin F. Perry: South Carolina Unionist* (Durham, 1946), p. 397.
10. December 27, 1865.
11. Saxton to Howard, September 9, 1865, Bureau Records, Box 728-A.

ers, including agents of the Bureau, were continuing to implant wild ideas in the minds of the Negroes. One newspaper spoke contemptuously of "the emissaries of abolitionism" who were exercising "a nefarious influence" among the freedmen by filling them with false hopes about free land.[12] Another, in a sweeping indictment of Yankees in general, asserted: "We do not say that all Northern men who come South are of the class alluded to, but we do say that all who prowl through the country, teaching the negroes that they are ill-used by the Southern people—that the lands are to be given to the colored people on any terms whatever . . . —that they can redress the supposed wrongs of blacks—and the like pretences of special friendship and regard, are of the vilest and meanest sect that ever disgraced the annals of civilization."[13]

White hostility toward the Bureau was further inflamed by its work in trying to regulate the conditions of labor under which the freedmen were to be employed, an undertaking which touched the very nerve center of race relations. The real problem, of course, lay not so much in what the Bureau did or failed to do, but in the hard necessity of both races having to unlearn more than two hundred years of attitude, custom, and habit as fashioned by slavery—a change which time, experience, and mutual good-will alone could even partially produce. Most of the whites in 1865 clearly felt that labor relations, like the broader question of race relations, could be established within the traditional framework, while many of the freedmen just as clearly believed that emancipation was going to usher in some kind of millenium. On the one hand, then, it was inevitable that the Bureau, as it sought to define and regulate a new system of labor contracts, would arouse the resentment as well as certain racial fears of the whites; on the other, it was nearly as inevitable that it would, in time, disappoint those freedmen who looked to it for the fulfillment of unrealizable hopes. To the whole picture, finally, must be added the utopian beliefs of many Bureau agents who initially felt that the whole question could be solved easily

12. Charleston *Courier*, May 25 and July 1, 1866.
13. Columbia *Daily Phoenix*, June 4, 1867. For additional indications of white hostility toward the Bureau over the land question, see the long letter of James L. Orr to President Johnson, as printed in the Charleston *Courier*, February 3, 1866, and D. E. Huger Smith, *A Charlestonian's Recollections, 1846-1913* (Charleston, 1950), pp. 119-26.

and in short order if both races would simply decide to adjust to the new realities.

The disappointing harvest of 1865 did nothing to improve understanding among the three groups involved. One rural weekly, for example, with only thinly-veiled resentment towards the role of the Bureau in the new labor arrangement, noted with some apparent grim satisfaction that among the Negroes of the vicinity on New Year's Day, 1866, poverty had been everywhere apparent. "Deep concern, if not disappointment," the editor observed, "seemed to be written upon countenances which were wont to be redolent with satisfaction, happiness and glee. Already the sweets of *glorious freedom* were turning bitter to their lips." With some measure of sarcasm the editorial then asked, "And *who* is his friend *now?* Unless those who have *oppressed* and *injured* him from his birth take him in, he, and his wife, and his children, must suffer and die." And yet, concluded the journal, such "Negrophilists" as Mansfield French, the Bureau's agent in the area, "continue to live and move and have a being—and flourish!"[14]

One action which many whites found especially galling was that of some Bureau officials who, at harvest time, set aside contracts which they viewed as unjust to the workers, even though the contract terms had been properly approved in the beginning of the year by an authorized person. Governor James L. Orr, as did other white spokesmen, strongly protested "in the name of common justice" against such arbitrary practice.[15] Still another Bureau policy which white planters found objectionable was a fee system which prevailed in the beginning as a means of financing the administration of the labor contract system. Agents were authorized to charge the employer a fee of up to fifty cents per worker employed for approving a labor contract. Such a practice, in white opinion, not only worked an economic hardship upon the landowners, but also enriched agents and officers at their expense. One Bureau official, for example, was reported to have realized an income of two thousand dollars in such fees during one year alone.[16] The decision of General Howard to

14. Sumter *Watchman,* January 10, 1866.
15. James L. Orr to Scott, December 6, 1866, Bureau Records, S. C., Box 476.
16. James L. Orr to Scott, May 12, 1866, Bureau Records, S. C., Box 476.

abolish the practice in 1866 was prompted, in all probability, by the volume and strength of white objection to it.

There was, in fact, little about the Bureau's labor program that escaped criticism from white spokesmen. Some expressed the belief that the work of the agency was opening "an irreconcilable antagonism between the former owner and the freed slave" as the freedman was prompted to believe that "the white community are his natural enemies." The Negro, declared the spokesman, was being taught "that every concession of remuneration" by his employer "is only so much wrung from the white man by compulsion."[17] Others charged that the Bureau's interference had such an unsettling effect on Negro workers that "the day is not far distant when all will have to seek out white labor."[18] One newspaper, noting that Kershaw county had never had a regular office of the Bureau established within its limits, commented, "This County is referred to as the most prosperous one in the State, so far as the good behavior and industry of the freedmen is concerned."[19] Another declared that, by its very presence, the Bureau encouraged "the ignorant and the indolent" to neglect their work and flock to headquarters with a great volume of trivial complaints.[20] Still other whites protested that freedmen were allowed to violate their contracts with impunity, while the employer was punished for alleged violations. The editor of a rural weekly, speaking of the Bureau, flatly asserted, "It has done the negro more harm than can ever be repaired." He went on to characterize its officials as "negrophilists, professed humanitarians, and sharp speculating characters" about whose garments "the stench of the grave yard always hangs."[21]

Relentlessly and from every direction, white spokesmen kept up their barrage of criticism towards the Bureau's labor policy— less, one feels, because of the actual flaws in the program than because of the potential threat which it posed to the traditional pattern of race relations. Repeatedly they proclaimed that the only ones who knew and understood the Negro were the native

17. Yorkville *Inquirer*, January 25, 1866.
18. Sumter *Watchman*, May 30, 1866.
19. Columbia *Daily Phoenix*, May 30, 1866.
20. Yorkville *Inquirer*, January 18, 1866.
21. Sumter *Watchman*, December 20, 1865. See also the Charleston *Daily News*, August 4 and 15, 1866, and January 21, 1867; Fairfield *Herald*, January 30, 1867; and Charleston *Courier*, June 6, 1866.

whites and that, until they had the right, free from outside interference, to control his employment, agricultural life in the state
could be neither sound nor productive. With a bit of humor one
editor expressed a widespread view in writing: "We hope the
day is not far distant when we shall be able to say with the little
black urchin in Richmond the other day when he saw an officer
of the Freedmen's Bureau slip and fall down on the frozen street.
'Dar now—de Freedmen's Buro done busted!' "[22]

Perhaps the most stinging attack made upon the Bureau by
any white spokesman was that by Judge A. P. Aldrich in his
charge to a grand jury in 1866. In scathing terms he declared:

> We are greatly embarrassed in the management of our
> domestic affairs by the presence and interference of the
> Freedmen's Bureau. I believe if the difficult and delicate
> problem of organizing the labor of our former slaves was
> entirely left to us, who once owned the freedmen, under-
> stand their character and feel for their condition, things
> would be so managed as to enable us, very soon, to regain
> their confidence and to infuse into their minds a feeling of
> security and protection. . . . But, as matters now stand, dis-
> trust is engendered, the freedmen are taught to be sus-
> picious of their old masters—to believe that their interests
> are antagonistic—and encouraged to distrust their counsel,
> advice and aid; all of which would soon cease, if this in-
> terested and prejudiced Bureau was removed. It is a great,
> useless, expensive and mischevious machinery, which seems
> to be kept up simply to grind taxes out of the people for the
> support of cunning politicians, excited lunatics and political
> preachers.[23]

Yet not even such attacks as these exhausted the grievances
of the whites against the Bureau. They also sharply criticized
the agency's relief program among the freedmen, claiming that
by its distribution of food, clothing, and supplies it encouraged
laziness, fostered the hope of getting something for nothing, and
heightened the "natural" tendency of the Negroes toward

22. Fairfield *Herald*, January 16, 1867.
23. *Ibid.*, October 10, 1866. It might be noted, on the other hand, that
on rare occasions a highly exceptional white could be found endorsing the
policy of the Bureau. One at Bennettsville declared his belief that through
the free labor system, "our desolated South will soon rise again from its
ruins." C. W. Dudley to B. F. Whittemore, January 22, 1866, Bureau
Records, S. C., Box 476.

thievery, vagrancy, and vice.[24] Some of the freedmen, according to one editor, "really fancy that they will never have to work again—that they have nothing to do save to sing and to dance, and to eat the food, and wear the clothes which will be provided for them by the Freedmen's Bureau." In his opinion, they viewed the Bureau "as a gigantic storehouse, created for their individual ease and comfort, out of which is to come at their bid all that is pleasant for them." He concluded: "The welfare and prosperity of the black race depends, in a great measure, on the abolition of the Freedmen's Bureau—the peace, the policy, the convenience of the white race equally demand it."[25] Even a group of ministers in the state's capital, representing a charitable creed, were prompted to deplore the program of charity by the Bureau, terming its work one that had done "enormous evil in the land by rendering a class whose proclivities are to idleness and vagrancy, more idle and vagrant." Declaring that the agency had created "a race of paupers," the statement of the group went on to sound an ominous note: "An idle vagabond, with the undefined impression upon his mind that the property of his late master is somehow to pass into his possession, the negro will take by stealth or violence that which he cannot earn, and so the war of races will begin."[26] In later years another spokesman, referring to the Bureau's program of relief for the freedmen, could declare that "by feeding them in idleness, and putting the worst ideas in their heads" the Bureau had become such "an abomination" that the Federal government "abolished it as soon as it discovered its mistake in creating it."[27]

Another of the Bureau's programs which came under fire by the whites was its work in the realm of Negro education. Native critics, it would seem, objected less to schooling as such for the freedmen than to what they regarded as the corrupting influence of Northern teachers among them. It was not uncommon, for example, for planters to establish schools for the education of the children of their workers, or for native whites to become

24. For a typical expression of this view, see the Charleston *Mercury*, August 10, 1867.
25. Sumter *Watchman*, November 1, 1865.
26. "The Future of the Freedmen," *The Southern Presbyterian Review*, XIX (1868), 286.
27. A. Toomer Porter, *Led On! Step by Step* (New York, 1899), p. 194.

teachers in such schools.[28] One white spokesman expressed a typical view in urging his fellow-citizens to give more support to the cause of Negro schooling, declaring that "if we educate the black man, allow him to read, speak, hear speeches, vote and exercise the privileges of a FREE MAN, it derogates nothing from our character, . . . but raises him *towards a level*, at least, with us."[29] White objection to Negro schooling appears, then, to have stemmed from causes other than opposition to education per se. Some certainly resented the fact that education was being provided for the freedmen and not for the whites, except at the price of their belief in segregation. Confided a Charlestonian to his diary, after the city's schools came to be used for Negro children: "I suppose the . . . buildings will be kept until the little *nigger* race shall be prepared to enter College, whilst our poorer white children are growing up in Ignorance and vice."[30] Other whites opposed Negro schooling because, in the words of a leading newspaper, "the Northern people, under the auspices of the Government, and the immediate direction of that incubus, the Freedmen's Bureau" had established schools in which Northern teachers "maligned and traduced the Southern people" and taught "insolence and hatred more than anything else."[31]

What had been mainly opposition and protest ripened into strong hostility in 1867, as the freedmen acquired political rights under the Radical Reconstruction program. Native whites came increasingly to believe—occasionally with cause—that the schools were being used to indoctrinate the students with the beliefs and program of the Republican party. One spokesman, expressing a typical view, declared, "The sentiments which these Northern 'New Lights' are endeavoring to instill into the minds of our colored people are to the last degree pernicious to their best interest. . . . And I believe . . . that if those pernicious principles are persisted in, the day is not distant when we shall see thousands of our colored people wandering through the country without employment, food, raiment, or homes, and our ears will be-

28. Typical instances may be found in the Fairfield *Herald*, July 17, 1867; Sumter *Watchman*, June 5, 1867; and Columbia *Daily Phoenix*, July 2 and September 3, 1867.

29. *Keowee Courier*, April 27, 1867.

30. Entry of June 19, 1866, MS. diary of Jacob Schirmer, S. C. Historical Society, Charleston.

31. Columbia *Daily Phoenix*, September 21, 1866.

come familiarized with tales of murder, robbery, and burning."
The solution, the writer believed, was for native whites to take
"the mental and moral development" of the freedmen into their
own hands and "so occupy the ground as to leave no room for the
ingress of these Northern moths into the social hive." He concluded: "Now is the time to act; before another twelve-month
hundreds of Northern teachers will be pouring into our country,
and if they continue as they have begun we may well tremble for
our safety, and many of our people will be called to suffer . . .
for their sad dereliction in so important a matter."[32] In a similar
vein, another spokesman proclaimed: "We want teachers . . .
taught among us, *and of us,* who . . . will leave politics outside
of the school-room doors. . . ."[33] An editor, urging the whites
of the state to give more money and energy to education of the
freedmen, declared: "The colored man is a power in the State
government. . . . Should he not then be educated? And should
not his education be such as would tend to soften down and
harmonize the differences which have grown out of past political
antagonism? This can only be effected through the agency of
Southern teachers."[34]

White charges of political indoctrination against the teachers
in Bureau-sponsored schools broadened during 1867 and 1868 to
include officers and agents as well. As the freedmen became
more active in the politics of the time, most whites became
wholly convinced that Bureau officials were using their influence
to organize them in support of the Radical Republican cause.
Said one, in reference to the Bureau, "The radicals have seized
this institution and made it a political engine, by the means of
which they intend to carry out their doctrine of equality of the
races, universal suffrage, &c."[35] Another characterized the Bureau as "nothing more or less than a gigantic Radical party
machine" and General Howard as "a natural fanatic—one of the
psalm-singing sort from New England."[36]

The issue of political activity, without doubt, was the one

32. *Keowee Courier,* June 9, 1866.
33. Columbia *Daily Phoenix,* April 3, 1867. See also the Yorkville
Inquirer, July 26, 1866, and the Sumter *Watchman,* June 5, 1867.
34. *Keowee Courier,* April 22, 1870.
35. Columbia *Daily Phoenix,* August 14, 1866. See also the Camden
Journal, January 23, 1868.
36. Newberry *Herald,* August 28, 1867.

which did most to embitter the whites towards the Bureau, yet by no means did this exhaust their charges. The Bureau, among other things, was characterized "as a kind of sinecure for abolition pets to creep into . . . , draw pay, and do little or nothing beneficial to the darkies."[37] Most agents and officers, according to one critic, were "money-making philanthropists" who attached themselves to a mercenary endeavor like "a vulture to a dead carcass."[38] Another spokesman, commenting upon General Howard's order which forbade agents to engage in planting operations on the side, expressed the hope that the prohibition might be broadened to include "those running saw-mills, and otherwise speculating in and profiting by the 'sweat of the freedmen's face.'"[39] An editor of a rural weekly, reckoning that the Bureau had cost taxpayers from fifteen to twenty million dollars, charged that the bulk of this amount had gone into the pockets of officers and agents, and not towards the welfare of the Negro. "It is a very easy thing for a Radical to appear as the friend of the colored people when he is getting a good salary for it," he concluded.[40] Some whites also saw in the creation of the Bureau a dangerous development towards centralized power in Washington that posed an ominous threat to states' rights and individual liberties; unchecked, the trend foretold "a sorrowful end of that free Government . . . handed down by the fathers."[41]

On the whole, white attacks upon the Bureau were confined to the world of words; mainly the weapons were thundering protests and angry denunciations. Occasionally, however, hostility took the form of abuse and threats against the individual agent. At Kingstree, for example, local feeling against the Bureau officer ran so high that a garrison of troops had to be stationed there for his protection.[42] A similar instance occurred in Abbeville, where the agent, W. F. DeKnight, had the misfortune to incur the wrath of one of the state's more prominent and voluble planters, D. Wyatt Aiken. Aiken charged DeKnight with

37. Yorkville *Inquirer,* September 13, 1866.
38. Sumter *Watchman,* December 20, 1865.
39. Columbia *Daily Phoenix,* May 23, 1866.
40. Abbeville *Banner,* September 30, 1868.
41. Sumter *Watchman,* September 25, 1867. See also the Columbia *Daily Phoenix,* June 23, 1866.
42. Scott to James L. Orr, December 17, 1866, "Freedmen's File," S. C. Historical Commission.

using his office to promote the Republican cause among the freedmen, and accused him of "telling the Negroes a lot of damned lies." Local feeling against DeKnight reached fever pitch after Aiken somehow acquired and published a copy of the agent's confidential report in which he had called conditions in the county deplorable and characterized the freedmen as "a great deal worse off . . . than when they were slaves." The resulting uproar, according to DeKnight, produced a situation in which "I may be shot down by some drunken, if not by a sober scoundrel, even here in my own office."[43]

But instances such as these were highly exceptional. In general whites expressed their hostility against the Bureau with a relentless verbal attack, charging it with serving political ends; with encouraging the freedmen in idleness; with fostering racial ill-will; with being meddlesome, unjust, partisan, and wasteful. Yet it seems clear that these were mainly the expression of a deeper and broader fear of the whites, a fear that the ultimate effect of the Bureau would be to disrupt race relations and so endanger white supremacy. City leaders of Charleston, for example, in discussing the Bureau with General Howard in the fall of 1865, dwelt at some length on this point, objecting to the agency on the ground that "the social relations of the people are placed under the . . . caprices of the different officers."[44] A leading newspaper made much the same protest, terming the Bureau "a common disturber of the relations of the two races."[45] Another voiced a similar view in remarking that, "The fatal element of disorder consists in this—that it is an arbitrary organization—supported by the bayonet—for the benefit of one portion of the people against another. It avows and perpetuates antagonism and conflict."[46] In one of the harshest indictments ever penned against the Bureau, the Charleston *Mercury* declared:

It consists of an army of malignant Southern haters, negro fanatics, and needy adventurers, backed in their power by the army of the United States. They have done more to breed an irradicable [*sic*] alienation of the people of the Southern States, from the people of the Northern States, than the war

43. W. F. DeKnight to H. Neide, September 25 and 30, 1868, Bureau Records, S. C., Box 480; Abbeville *Banner*, September 30, 1868.
44. Charleston *Courier*, October 23, 1865.
45. *Ibid.*, January 2, 1868.
46. Charleston *Mercury*, December 22, 1866.

itself. It is they who have got up the Union Leagues amongst the negroes, and have made them enemies of the white race. It is they who are the instruments of the Radical party, to Africanize the South, and to put the white man under the negro. It is they, who have indoctrinated the negro with the idea, that to take the white man's land is their right; and to kill him is a righteous duty. All the public riots, and not a few of the private murders perpetrated by the negroes on the white people, are traceable directly to the incendiary teachings of some of the agents of this bureau. Everywhere its influence, with but few exceptions, has been adverse to the peace of the country, or to any steady or efficient industry amongst the blacks.[47]

In a similar spirit the Confederate hero and plantation aristocrat, Wade Hampton, wrote a long letter to President Johnson about the Bureau. Terming it "that incubus" and "Hydra-headed monster," he asserted that it had been used "by the basest men, for the purpose of swindling the negro, plundering the white man and defrauding the Government." In a sweeping denunciation he concluded: "*There may* be an honest man connected with the Bureau, but I fear that the commissioners sent by your Excellency [Generals Steedman and Fullerton] to probe the rottenness of this cancer will find their search for such as fruitless as was that of the Cynic of old."[48]

But such angry denunciations are misleading if taken at face value to represent the whole attitude of whites towards the Bureau. When one looks more closely, he finds a curious paradox involved. On the one hand white spokesmen repeatedly, and sometimes savagely, attacked the Bureau as an institution; on the other, whites within a given community often found the individual agent a respectable and even likeable human being. For example, one officer of considerable experience reported in 1867 that the people of Marion county had always treated him with courtesy; in another instance, an agent developed such

47. *Ibid.*, December 17, 1867. See also the Yorkville *Inquirer*, January 25, 1866, and Sumter *Watchman*, December 13, 1865.

48. Hampton to Johnson, undated, 1866, MS., Wade Hampton Collection, South Caroliniana Library, University of South Carolina. In the county of Darlington, according to an agent there, the hostility towards the Bureau and Northerners in general was so strong that most of the people "were miniature Hamilcars, bringing up their 'Hannibals.'" George Pingree to Scott, September 24, 1867, Bureau Records, S. C., Vol. 177.

friendly relations with the white community of Columbia that Assistant Commissioner Scott felt it necessary to admonish him for "hobnobbing" with the whites, lest he lose the respect and confidence of the Negroes.[49] The urbane and gifted John W. De Forest wrote that in Greenville, despite occasional instances of discourtesy, he found a general air of hospitality that included numerous invitations to breakfasts, dinners, teas, and picnics.[50] And in another case, a group of leading citizens, upon learning that the local Bureau officer was to be transferred elsewhere, petitioned for his retention there. "In our judgment," they wrote, "his course has been approved by all fair minded men, both white and black. . . ."[51]

Moreover, on numerous occasions military officers, many of whom were also serving as Bureau agents, were strongly commended by the whites of the community. In one case the local paper described the officer as one who had served with "such discretion and impartiality" as to have commanded the esteem and respect of all classes of our people."[52] In another instance, the officer was characterized as a man of "unwearied patience and dignity" whose "evident desire to administer Justice" was so highly regarded that the members of the local bar were preparing a written testimonial to his "official worth and merit."[53] In Charleston the *Courier* praised an officer there for being "the true type of the gallant soldier and American gentleman."[54] And in Anderson the retiring commander took the unusual step of publishing a card of appreciation in which he said he had found the citizens "a friendly and quiet people."[55]

Most surprising of all, perhaps, were the endorsements given by various whites to the administration of Assistant Commissioner Robert K. Scott. The Charleston *Daily News,* for example, declared: "The writer . . . freely admits the integrity of the purpose and propriety of deportment of General Scott,"

49. Scott to W. J. Harkisheimer, August 7, 1867, Bureau Records, S. C., Box 518.
50. De Forest, *A Union Officer,* p. 46.
51. Group of Citizens to Scott, undated, Bureau Records, S. C., Box 480.
52. Orangeburg *News,* June 20, 1868.
53. Sumter *Watchman,* November 15, 1865.
54. September 14, 1865.
55. Columbia *Daily Phoenix,* May 10, 1866. For other examples see the Sumter *Watchman,* August 29, 1866, and September 4, 1867; Newberry *Herald,* August 18, 1865, and June 27, 1866.

under whose direction the Bureau, "utterly odious under the conduct of his predecessor," had become "tolerable, and by contrast, most agreeable."[56] Another paper, while disclaiming any especial regard for the Bureau, commended Scott for his "judgment and sound discretion" in conducting the agency's affairs and for his efforts to direct it "for the benefit of those for whom it was designed."[57] A still more striking example of the general regard for the assistant commissioner was the action of two groups of distinguished white spokesmen when they learned that he was scheduled to be mustered out of service at the end of 1867. They sent petitions to President Johnson asking for Scott's retention, at least until plans for the new planting year were complete; one termed his general administration "beneficial" and another declared: "Genl. Scott is well and favorably known to both Freedmen and Planters, both of whom have full confidence in his ability and integrity of purpose."[58]

This ambivalence in white attitudes towards the Bureau was noted at the time by Whitelaw Reid, the astute observer touring the South in 1865 and 1866. Commenting upon it, he wrote: "In most cases, the hostility to the Freedman's Bureau seemed to be general in its nature, not specific. Men regarded it as tyrannical and humiliating that Government hirelings should be sent among them to supervise their relations with their old slaves; but in practice, they were very glad of the supervision. It was a degrading system, they argued, but, so long as it existed, the negroes could not be controlled except by the favor of the Bureau agents. . . . When the agents were removed from this prevailing respect for their powers, few opportunities were lost to show them the estimation in which they were held."[59]

And so the paradox stands. On the one hand white critics and spokesmen waged a relentless attack against the Bureau as an institution, questioning its need, doubting its purpose, and denying its worth; they professed to view it as an intruder, a usurper, and an added distraction in an already-distracted society. On the other hand, in numerous instances they willingly recognized and

56. As reprinted in the Columbia *Daily Phoenix*, June 5, 1866.
57. Columbia *Daily Phoenix*, December 25, 1867.
58. Citizens to President Johnson, August 24 and December 4, 1867, Bureau Records, Box 786; Citizens to Johnson, undated, MS., Scott Papers.
59. *After the War: A Southern Tour* (New York, 1866), p. 577.

paid tribute to the merit of the individual Bureau official. Thus, white hostility towards the Bureau in South Carolina was never so uniform nor so unqualified as myth and folklore of the state would later portray it. Though such a contradiction in attitudes is easier to describe than explain, still two or three things seem clear. One is that much of the criticism of the Bureau sprang more from a fear that its work would endanger white supremacy than from any concern with its actual faults. In tone as well as spirit, so many of the charges against the agency clearly suggest this to be the case, especially once the freedmen had become politically active. Another consideration is that some of the animus towards the Bureau was a by-product of the general anti-Northern feeling that prevailed in the state. Finally, many whites convinced themselves that the Bureau as an institution was somehow different from the individuals who made it up. Thus, they could angrily denounce the agency and its policies, while at the same time finding much to praise about the individual officers and agents themselves. But over the years this latter fact never managed to find its way into the folklore of the state. To the extent that legend and myth have obscured this truth, so much has the cause of historical justice towards the Bureau in South Carolina been distorted.

As the godchild of war and strife, the Bureau seems to have been marked by fate for a stormy life. Throughout its career, controversy was its almost constant companion. Its purposes were often the subject of sharp debate and its work in the field was under incessant attack by its critics. Even at the end it would not be allowed to expire quietly. Because of various charges made against the agency, a congressional committee in 1870 undertook a sweeping investigation into its record. At the close of the inquiry the Democratic minority on the committee concluded that the charges of incompetence and dereliction of duty had been proved against General Howard, and recommended that he be tried by court-martial. They were also convinced that his subordinates shared his guilt; under the guise of friendship and counsel, they declared, agents and officers had "misled, duped, . . . debauched, and then swindled the ignorant negroes." Howard and other Bureau officials, the minority concluded, could not forever "escape a just retribution for their hypocrisy and their crimes."[1]

But if the Democratic minority were persuaded that the Bureau had served no worthwhile purpose, the Republican majority were even more confident about the good it had accomplished. In a ringing endorsement they wrote: "Success! The world can point to nothing like it in all the history of emancipation. No thirteen millions of dollars were ever more wisely spent. . . . Scoffed at like a thing of shame, often struck and sorely wounded, sometimes in the house of its friends, apologized for rather than defended; yet with God on its side, the Freedmen's Bureau has triumphed; civilization has received a new impulse, and the friends of humanity may well rejoice."[2]

Such a conflict of view not only reflected the division of opinion of the day; it also anticipated the judgment of the fu-

1. *House Reports*, 41 Cong., 2 Sess., no. 121 (serial 1438), pp. 54-55.
2. *Ibid.*, p. 20.

ture, for even today, a century after the Bureau's time, its merits remain a matter of dispute. There are those who see it as an abused and misunderstood institution which performed a meaningful and needed service;[3] there are others who believe that, by feeding the flames of racial discord, the Bureau "cancelled out much of the good it had otherwise accomplished for the Negro and the nation."[4] Historians of the present generation, thus, seem little more likely to reach a consensus in the matter than the observers of a hundred years ago.

Though the question of the Bureau's over-all worth is neither simple nor easy to answer, the statistics concerning its work in the South are clear enough. Between the time of its creation and the close of 1868, it issued more than twenty-one million rations, established over forty hospitals, treated nearly half a million cases of illness, provided free transportation to more than thirty thousand persons dislocated by war, and supervised hundreds of thousands of labor contracts. It also sought to transform the landless mass of freedmen into owners of the soil; and though it failed at last, it did succeed in helping some to obtain farms under the Southern Homestead Act. In addition, it gave extensive support to the cause of Negro schooling, working closely with private agencies in maintaining thousands of schools, thereby enabling tens of thousands of freedmen to gain at least the rudiments of an education.

The comparative figures for South Carolina are equally impressive. There, during the three and a half years of its effective operation, the Bureau issued something like three million rations to the freedmen and white refugees of the state, in addition to providing $300,000 worth of supplies under the crop-lien program of 1868; supplied medical care to about 175,000 persons, and free transportation to at least 5,000 individuals; supervised perhaps 300,000 labor contracts; arbitrated countless thousands of complaints and quarrels between Negroes and whites; and gave substantial help in maintaining an educational system that averaged 85 schools a year with an enrollment of about 100,000

3. See John and La Wanda Cox, "General O. O. Howard and the 'Misrepresented Bureau,'" *Journal of Southern History*, XIX (November, 1953), 427-56.

4. George R. Bentley, *A History of the Freedmen's Bureau* (Philadelphia, 1955), p. 214.

students. Moreover, by its very presence and concern it made an intangible yet important contribution towards helping the Negro to walk in greater dignity as a free man.

The figures themselves tell of both the variety and scope of the Bureau's endeavor. But in a sense they beg the larger question of whether what was done was all that might have been done with the means at hand, and whether the legacy of the Bureau is to be found more in its deeds than in its failures. The answer to such questions must be sought as much in the context of time and circumstance in which it labored as in the substance of its achievement; as much, in other words, in conditions over which it had little control as in those over which it had much.

One such consideration is that relating to manpower resources. Almost from the beginning the Bureau in South Carolina had to labor under the handicap of a personnel shortage so severe that it could never adequately serve the needs demanded by its responsibilities. Especially was this true during its first and most critical year of existence, for once the President had directed the Bureau to restore confiscated property to its original white owners, the agency had no assured income on which to draw. And though the financial situation grew brighter after Congress in 1866 provided a two-year appropriation, still the funds available for recruiting officers and agents were never commensurate with the needs. At no time were the field forces in South Carolina large enough to station even one agent in each county. Throughout the whole of the Bureau's life, there were thousands of freedmen who probably never even saw an official of the agency, and who certainly never felt its influence to any degree.

Allied somewhat to this consideration was the awkwardness which characterized the relationship between the Bureau and the military forces in the state. For one thing, many Bureau subordinates were also army officers whose first loyalty was to their military superiors and not to the assistant commissioner; many of them, moreover, felt little sympathy for the work of the Bureau and made slight effort to disguise the fact. In addition, the assignment and use of troops, without which the Bureau could not possibly enforce many of its decisions, remained an exclusive prerogative of military commanders, who more than once curtly refused the request of an agent for troops to be detached on Bureau business.

Understaffed, underfinanced, and sometimes undercut by military will, the Bureau could do little more than approximate the potential that lay within it for advancing the general welfare of the freedmen. The fervor of its founders and the good wishes of its supporters were poor substitutes for the actual resources needed in meeting the large and complex challenge it had to face. In South Carolina the agency never became strong enough in either personnel or financial support to render a service equal to the needs of those for whom it was created. The real test of the Bureau's worth is to be found more in the meaning it helped to give freedom for a Negro in some remote county of the state than in all the aims of Congress or the directives of General Howard. And here it stumbled badly, though less because its feet were misdirected than because they were hobbled by its sponsors.

Even more basic than any of these factors in limiting the Bureau's effectiveness was its anomalous position in American society of the mid-nineteenth century. In a real sense it did not belong to the America of its day. As an attempt, however limited, at social engineering and an expression, however tentative, at social planning by government, it was contrary to both history and tradition in the nation's development. As the history of the Bureau all too clearly shows, Americans of the day were unwilling to support, on any large scale or over any sustained span of time, an endeavor which called for direct and active intervention in the affairs of society by Federal authority. Nowhere did this truth find more vigorous expression than in the message of President Johnson accompanying his veto of the Freedmen's Bureau bill of February, 1866. Commenting upon the provision of the bill which authorized the Bureau to assist refugees and freedmen in the areas of land, relief, and education, he declared:

> The Congress of the United States has never heretofore thought itself empowered to establish asylums beyond the limits of the District of Columbia, except for the benefit of our disabled soldiers and sailors. It has never founded schools for any class of our own people, not even for the orphans of those who have fallen in the defense of the Union, but has left the care of education to the much more

competent and efficient control of the States, of communities, or private associations, and of individuals. It has never deemed itself authorized to expend the public money for the rent or purchase of homes for the thousands, not to say millions, of the white race who are honestly toiling from day to day for their subsistence. A system for the support of indigent persons in the United States was never contemplated by the authors of the Constitution; nor can any good reason be advanced why, as a permanent establishment, it should be founded for one class or color of our people more than another. Pending the war many refugees and freedmen received support from the Government, but it was never intended that they should thenceforth be fed, clothed, educated, and sheltered by the United States.[5]

Though Johnson was seldom in tune with the national temper during the troubled years of Reconstruction, in this point of view, at least, he was probably closer to the basic mood and attitude of the nation about governmental authority and right than were his political enemies. In this sense, it might be said that the Bureau was born seventy-five years too soon.

A final factor conditioning the Bureau's ultimate record was the brevity, along with the uncertainty, of its existence. Created originally to last for only one year beyond the end of the war, it labored throughout most of its initial months under the impression that it would be discontinued at the end of the first year. Then in the summer of 1866 its life was prolonged for two years more, and at the last moment, for another six months—a sum total of about three and a half years. Its creators either did not recognize or would not admit the paradox involved in their attitude towards the freedmen: either slavery had been a sound school of civilization in preparing the Negro for an easy transition to responsible citizenship, or else the ex-slave was going to need more time, money, and effort than could possibly be given in the short span of less than four years. Since slavery had been a thing far bigger than physical chains, it was naïve to believe that its undoing could be so simple a matter. There is still no reason to question the discerning judgment of W. E. B. Du Bois, the first

5. James D. Richardson (comp.), *A Compilation of the Messages and Papers of the Presidents, 1789-1902* (New York, 1897-1902), VI, 401.

serious scholar to recognize and extol the merits of the Bureau, when, more than half a century ago, he wrote:

> In a time of perfect calm, amid willing neighbors and streaming wealth, the social uplifting of four million slaves to an assured and self-sustaining place in the body politic and economic would have been a herculean task; but when to the inherent difficulties of so delicate and nice a social operation were added the spite and hate of conflict, the hell of war; when suspicion and cruelty were rife, and gaunt Hunger wept beside Bereavement,—in such a case, the work of any instrument of social regeneration was in large part foredoomed to failure.[6]

In South Carolina the judgment, at last, to be rendered is that the Bureau was a qualified failure. It is the verdict called for when the dimensions of the achievement are rigorously measured against those of the need; the former are so meager, the latter so large. But the fault lies less with the Bureau than with the nation, whose conviction about total freedom for the former slaves was not matched by a courage and commitment great enough to insure it. Thereby, an endeavor that might have proved to be at least the half-way house to freedom turned out instead to be merely the point of departure for a people to begin the lonely walk down a long road that would bend well into the twentieth century.

6. W. E. B. Du Bois, *Souls of Black Folk: Essays and Sketches* (Chicago, 1918), pp. 27-28.

These documents are located in the records of the Freedmen's Bureau (South Carolina), Appendix A in Box 483, Appendix B in Box 536, Appendix C in Box 533, and Appendix D in Box 520 and Box 516.

Appendix A: FORM FOR THE RESTORATION OF CONFISCATED PROPERTY HELD BY THE BUREAU

Richard H. Jenkins, an applicant for the restoration of his plantation on Wadmalaw Island, S. C., called "Rackett Hall," the same having been unoccupied during the past year and up to the 1st of Jan. 1866, except by one freedman who planted no crop, and being held by the Bureau of Refugees, Freedmen and Abandoned Lands, having conformed to the requirements of Circular No. 15 of said Bureau, dated Washington, D. C., Sept. 12, 1865, the aforesaid property is hereby restored to his possession.

The above instrument to be considered null and void unless the obligation herewith attached and subscribed to by said Richard H. Jenkins be faithfully and fully complied with.

All differences arising under this instrument and obligation are to be adjusted by the Board of Supervisors constituted by order of the Commissioner of the Bureau of Refugees, Freedmen and Abandoned Lands, dated Charleston, November 14, 1865.

· · · · · ·

The Undersigned, Richard H. Jenkins, does hereby solemnly promise and engage, that he will secure to the Refugees and Freedmen now resident on his Wadmalaw Island Estate, the crops of the past year, harvested or unharvested; also, that the said Refugees and Freedmen shall be allowed to remain at their present houses or other homes on the island, so long as the responsible Refugees and Freedmen (embracing parents, guardians, and other natural protectors) shall enter into contracts, by leases or for wages, in terms satisfactory to the Supervising Board.

Also, that the undersigned will take the proper steps to enter into contracts with the above described responsible Refugees and Freedmen, the latter being required on their part to enter into said contracts on or before the 15th day of February, 1866, or surrender their right to remain on the said estate, it being understood that if they are unwilling to contract after the expiration of said period, the Supervising Board is to aid in getting them homes and employment elsewhere.

Also, that the undersigned will take the proper steps to enter to schools sanctioned by the Supervising Board, or by the Bureau of Refugees, Freedmen and Abandoned Lands.

But nothing in this instrument shall be so construed as to relieve the above mentioned persons from the ordinary judicial consequences of crime and misdemeanor.

Neither the land owners nor the Refugees and Freedmen will be obligated by this instrument beyond one year from this date, unless the instrument is renewed.

Appendix B: FORM OF POSSESSORY TITLE TO SEA ISLAND LANDS UNDER SHERMAN'S ORDER

To All Whom It May Concern

Edisto Island, August 15th, 1865

George Owens, having selected for settlement forty acres of Land, on Theodore Belab's Place, pursuant to Special Field Orders, No. 15, Headquarters Military Division of the Mississippi, Savannah, Ga., Jan. 16, 1865; he has permission to hold and occupy the said Tract, subject to such regulations as may be established by proper authority; and all persons are prohibited from interfering with him in his possession of the same.

By command of

R. SAXTON

Brev't Maj. Gen., Ass't. Comm. S. C., Ga., and Fla.

Appendix C: APPOINTMENT OF A BUREAU AGENT IN 1865

Colonel E. A. Kozlay

Dear Sir:

You are hereby appointed Act'g. Sub. Ass't. Comm'r. of the

Bureau of Refugees, Freedmen and Abandoned Lands for the districts of Orangeburg and Barnwell, S. C.

I. I would respectfully invite your careful attention to the Orders and Circulars Issued by the Commissioner of the Bureau, and from these Headquarters. These will fully explain the duties expected of you by this Bureau. The persons under your charge must be protected in their rights and encouraged in their industry.

II. The following form of contract is adopted as applicable to the labor question, subject to the necessary modifications to meet individual and peculiar circumstances of contracting parties.

KNOW ALL MEN BY THESE PRESENTS, That ....
.................................., of the County of ...., State of ...., held and firmly bound to the United States of America in the sum of .... Dollars, for the payment of which .... bind .... Heirs, Executors and Administrators, firmly by these Presents in this Contract: That .... to furnish the persons whose names are subjoined (freed laborers), Quarters, Fuel, substantial and healthy Rations, all necessary Medical Attendance and Supplies in case of Sickness, and the amount set opposite their respective names per month, during the continuation of this Contract— the laborers to be paid in full before the final disposal of the crop which is to be raised by them on .... Plantation. . . .

III. When fair and equitable contracts are made, they must be kept both by employer and employed.

IV. This Bureau prescribes no fixed rates of wages, but leaves labor free to compete with other things of positive value in the market. Its duties are only to protect the laborer in his rights; and so long as no advantage is taken of the ignorance of freed people, to deprive them of a fair and reasonable compensation for their labor, any agreement that is satisfactory to both parties will be approved.

V. Wages must be secured by a lien on the crop raised. All contracts should be made in duplicate. . . . It is recommended, as far as possible, for the freedmen to cultivate the land for a share—one-half of the crop.

VI. Those who do not make contracts with the freedmen employed by them for the coming year, will be required to compensate them in such a manner as shall be satisfactory to the Assistant Commissioner.

VII. Parents must be required to provide for and support their children; and children, in turn, must support aged and helpless parents.

VIII. Circular No. 5, from the Commissioner, provides for the administration of Justice, and in certain cases commits it to your hands. It is desired that the civil magistrates in your county should administer justice, and you will allow them to do so so far as they are willing to act as Agents of this Bureau, and take for their method of procedure the laws now in force in the State, and applicable to free white citizens, receiving the testimony of freedpeople and other persons of color.

You are directed to propose to them to act as Agents of the Bureau in the administration of justice, under the above conditions. In the event of a refusal on their part, you then become the sole arbiter; and so far as the State laws make no distinction of color, your proceedings will be governed by them, excepting in the infliction of punishment by stripes or temporary reduction to slavery.

IX. Schools should be established and encouraged in every possible way. By education alone can the condition of this race be improved, and their liberty be made a blessing to them and to humanity.

The Freedmen's Bureau is but just starting on its mission, and we have no past experience to guide us in the performance of the peculiar and delicate duties which pertain to it; but rely in a great measure upon the earnestness, and good judgment and sense of justice of those who have its interests in charge. Let us strive to conduct its affairs that it shall be a power in our country for good and a blessing to those in whose interests it was established. . . .

R. SAXTON

Appendix D: TYPICAL LABOR CONTRACTS

August 5, 1865

This Agreement entered into between E. D. & L. R. Wright of the one part, and the Freedmen and Women of J. D. Wright's (deceased) plantation of the other part, Witnesseth:

That the latter agree, for the remainder of the present year, to reside upon and devote their labor to the cultivation of the Plantation of the former. And they further agree, that they will in all respects, conform to such reasonable and necessary plantation rules and regulations as E. D. & L. R. Wright may prescribe; that they will not keep any gun, pistol, or other offensive weapon, or leave the plantation without permission from their employer; that in all things connected with their duties as laborers on said plantation, they will yield prompt obedience to all and be quiet in their conduct, avoid drunkenness and other gross vices; that they will not misuse any of the Plantation Tools, or Agricultural Implements, or any Animals entrusted to their care, or any Boats, Flats, Carts, or Wagons; that they will give up at the expiration of this Contract all Tools &c, belonging to the Plantation, and in case any property, of any description belonging to the Plantation shall be willfully or through negligence destroyed or injured, the value of the Articles so destroyed shall be deducted from the portion of the Crops which the person or persons, so offending, shall be entitled to receive under this Contract.

Any deviations from the condition of the foregoing Contract, may, upon sufficient proof, be punished with dismissal from the Plantation or in such other manner as may be determined by the Provost Court; and the person or persons so dismissed, shall forfeit the whole, or a part of his, her or their portion of the crop, as the Court may decide.

In consideration of the foregoing Services duly performed, E. D. and L. R. Wright agree, after deducting seventy five bushels of Corn for each work Animal, exclusively used in cultivating the Crops for the present year; and the amount of Cotton necessary to pay for Bagging and Rope, to turn over to the said Freedmen and Women, one half of the remaining Cotton, Corn, Rice,

Peas, Potatoes, made this season. They further agree to furnish the usual rations until the Contract is performed.

All Cotton Seed produced on the Plantation is to be reserved for the use of the Plantation. The Freedmen, Women and Children, are to be treated in a manner consistent with their freedom. Necessary medical attention will be furnished as heretofore.

Any deviation from the conditions of this Contract upon the part of the said E. D. & L. R. Wright or their Agent or Agents shall be punished in such manner as may be determined by a Provost Court, or a Military Commission. This agreement to continue till the first day of January 1866.

· · · · · ·

April 15, 1868

I. Said Freedmen & Women agree to hire their time as Laborers on El Dorado Plantation from date of this contract until the expiration of the year or such time as the crop be prepared & shipped for market. They agree to conduct themselves civilly & honestly, & faithfully to perform such labour as may be required of them by their employer or his agent during their term of service; to obey all orders that may be given them & to perform the tasks heretofore required as their daily work; when tasks cannot be assigned, they agree to labour ten hours per day; they further agree not to absent themselves during work hours without the consent of their employer or his agent.

II. For every day's absence from labour, the labourer shall forfeit fifty cts. unless it be on account of weather; for absence without leave or persistent disobedience of orders if repeated three times, the offender shall be subject to dismissal from the plantation with forfeiture to inure to the benefit of employer & employees in proportion to their relative shares. Hired labor to be paid for from forfeiture.

III. Said Freedmen & Women agree to take good care of all tools & implements used upon the plantation; to be kind & gentle to work animals entrusted to their care, & to be responsible for any damage done either to animals or implements while in their hands, that may arise from carelessness or neglect.

IV. Said Thomas Pinckney agrees to furnish, on his part, a sufficient number of working animals & to feed them at his own expense; also such tools & implements as cannot be made upon the plantation.

V. For, & in consideration of the faithful performance of this agreement on the part of their [*sic*] employees, said Thomas Pinckney agrees to divide the crop with them as follows: one half of the highland crops, & one third of the Rice crop to be divided among the labourers in proportion to the amount of work done by each during the year, after repaying the advances and deductions to which each labourer may be liable; he further agrees to allow each labourer a half acre of Rice land to full hands, others in proportions, & a quarter of an acre of high land to plant for themselves, the product to be exclusively their own; to allow them to raise hogs & poultry, provided they be kept within their enclosures when required.

VI. The employer or his agent shall keep a book in which shall be entered all advances made; also, all absences, which book shall be received in evidence as merchants' books are received in courts of justice.

MANUSCRIPT RECORDS OF THE FREEDMEN'S BUREAU

The records of the Freedmen's Bureau, located in the War Records Office of the National Archives in Washington, were by far the most important collection of materials used in this study. They are divided into two broad groups, those relating to the central office of General Howard, and those pertaining to the field operations in the various states.

Those for South Carolina, occupying some forty-six linear feet of shelf space, are divided into box records, containing manuscripts of all kinds of reports and correspondence, and bound volumes. The boxes are numbered 470 through 545. Boxes 470-482 contain letters received by the assistant commissioner's office between 1865 and 1870. Generally, they are entered first by year, then by the initial letter of the name or office of the writer, and then numerically by the date of receipt. The remaining boxes contain a great variety of materials touching upon every phase of the Bureau's program. Especially important are boxes 502-536 which house the papers of the various subordinate offices throughout the state; they are shelved alphabetically by districts, beginning with "Aiken" and going through "Summerville." In them can be found such entries as letters received, labor contracts, proceedings of provost courts, and miscellaneous reports.

The bound volumes occupy slightly less than half of the total shelf space of the collection. Numbered 1 through 280, they complement, and sometimes duplicate, the boxed papers. Especially important are volumes 9 through 14, which contain copies of the letters sent by the assistant commissioner between 1865 and 1870, and volumes 26 through 32, which consist of general and specific orders issued from the assistant commissioner's office.

In addition to the box and book records, a number of loose and unclassified records are stored in the section. Examination of these turned up some items of real value.

Because the Bureau papers for many years were simply stored without care and without organization before being deposited in the National Archives, and because some of them were either destroyed or lost, the collection of records for South Carolina, voluminous though it is, remains incomplete. The records for 1865 especially are spotty. Yet by turning to the records of the central office the researcher can usually find there either copies of the various reports from the state or a synopsis of them. Boxes 732, 759, 778, 786, 1098 and 1099 of the central office records were especially useful in locating items bearing upon the Bureau's history for South Carolina.

A tool of great help in using the records was the excellent *Preliminary Checklist of the Records of the Bureau of Refugees, Freedmen, and Abandoned Lands, 1865-1872,* compiled in 1946 by Elizabeth Bethel, Sara Dunlap, and Lucille Pendell. By using it in the beginning the researcher can save himself many hours of time in locating the major categories of the record collection.

MANUSCRIPT COLLECTIONS

The most useful collection of private papers was that of O. O. Howard, located in the Bowdoin College Library; they contain a number of letters and other items of genuine value for the history of the Bureau in South Carolina. The hitherto-unused papers of Robert K. Scott were located in the possession of Mr. Robert Groschner of Detroit, Michigan, who generously allowed unconditional use of them. Most of Scott's letters between 1865 and 1876 have to do with his Civil War service or with his two terms as governor of South Carolina, but some fifty or sixty items that pertain to his tenure as assistant commissioner were found; a dozen or so of these were of real importance for this study.

At the South Carolina Historical Society in Charleston are three collections that yielded some helpful items. The letters of Caroline Howard Gilman convey some revealing comments upon social aspects of the period of Reconstruction, with occasional reference to the Bureau; a typescript copy of the papers of E. Mikell Whaley sheds some light on the question of freed labor; the multivolume diary of Jacob Schirmer, a longtime resident of Charleston and a keen observer of the contemporary scene, runs through the Reconstruction period and comprises a personal record that was full and engaging.

At the University of South Carolina the most useful papers were those of Wade Hampton. At the South Carolina Historical Commission were two collections that proved helpful: a letter book of Governor James L. Orr, and a file drawer marked "Freedmen's File" containing an assorted miscellany touching upon the Bureau's work. At the University of North Carolina the James L. Orr Papers proved to be of some value.

In the Library of Congress several collections proved useful. The Andrew Johnson Papers contain a number of items of help. The letters of J. Milton Hawks and his wife, both physicians in the Port Royal region, shed some light on the Bureau operations. A few papers of William H. Trescot reveal something of the reaction to the Bureau by a leading planter and spokesman from South Carolina. The letters of D. E. Sickles, Federal commander in the state for 1865-1866, also contain some items of importance for the history of the Bureau, especially concerning the relationship between the agency and the military forces.

NEWSPAPERS

Next to the Bureau Records themselves, contemporary newspapers of the state were of the greatest help for this study. All of the county weeklies were located in agricultural regions and consequently gave great attention to farming conditions and the work of the Bureau concerning them. Especially useful were the files of the Sumter *Watchman,* the Fairfield *Herald,* and the Yorkville *Inquirer.* Also of great help were the files of the two leading daily papers of the state, the Charleston *Courier* and the Columbia *Daily Phoenix.* The former gave extensive coverage to affairs in the coastal region while the latter did the same for the middle and upper sections of the state. Both carried in their columns a large number of directives and orders from Bureau offices; in some cases these were particularly valuable since the orders themselves were not among the Bureau records in the National Archives.

The following is a complete list of all newspapers used for the period of this study. Except where indicated, all were from the excellent collection of the Caroliniana Library at the University of South Carolina:

Anderson *Intelligencer*
Camden *Journal*
Charleston *Courier* (Charleston Library Society)
Charleston *Daily News* (Charleston Library Society)
Charleston *Mercury* (Charleston Library Society)
Columbia *Daily Phoenix*
Darlington *New Era*
Darlington *Southerner*
Edgefield *Advertiser*
The Free Press (microfilm, Howard University)
Keowee Courier
Laurensville *Herald*
Newberry *Herald*
Orangeburg *News*
South Carolina Leader (microfilm, Howard University)
Sumter *Watchman*
Unionville *Times*
Yorkville *Inquirer*

GOVERNMENT DOCUMENTS

A rich mine of information is contained in the large number of publications by the federal government. Most valuable for this study were the numerous documents and reports published by the two houses of Congress. Of these, the following issued under the authority of the House were particularly useful:

39th Congress, 1st session:
    House Executive Document No. 1 (serial 1249). "Report of the Secretary of War." 1866.
    House Executive Document No. 11 (serial 1255). "The Freedmen's Bureau." 1866.
    House Executive Documents Nos. 120-123 (serial 1263). "Report of Generals Steedman and Fullerton." 1866.
39th Congress, 2nd session:
    House Executive Document No. 1 (serial 1285). "Report of the Secretary of War." 1867.

House Executive Document No. 106 (serial 1293). "Rations." 1867.
40th Congress, 2nd session:
House Miscellaneous Document No. 81 (serial 1349). "Resolutions of the Constitutional Convention of South Carolina." 1868.
40th Congress, 3rd session:
House Executive Document No. 1 (serial 1367). "Report of Major General O. O. Howard." 1868.
41st Congress, 2nd session:
House Executive Document No. 1 (serial 1412). "Report of the Secretary of War." 1869.
House Executive Document No. 142 (serial 1417). "Report of Major General O. O. Howard." 1869.
House Executive Document No. 241 (serial 1425). "Bounties to Colored Soldiers." 1870.
41st Congress, 2nd session:
House Report No. 121 (serial 1438). "Charges Against General Howard." 1870.
41st Congress, 3rd session:
House Executive Document No. 1 (serial 1446). "Report of the Secretary of War." 1870.
42nd Congress, 2nd session:
House Executive Document No. 1 (serial 1503). "Report of the Secretary of War." 1871.
42nd Congress, 3rd session:
House Executive Document No. 109 (serial 1566). "Condition of the Affairs of the Freedmen's Bureau." 1873.
43rd Congress, 2nd session:
House Executive Document No. 59 (serial 1645). "Report of the Freedmen's Branch of the Adjutant-General's Office." 1874.
44th Congress, 1st session:
House Executive Document No. 144 (serial 1689). "Report of the Late Freedmen's Bureau for the Year Ending 30 June 1875." 1875.
Of those issued under the authority of the Senate, the following proved most useful:

39th Congress, 1st session:
Senate Executive Documents Nos. 2, 26, and 27 (serial 1237).
"Condition of the South." 1866.
Senate Executive Document No. 43 (serial 1238). "Report of
Benjamin C. Truman." 1866.
39th Congress, 2nd session:
Senate Executive Document No. 6 (serial 1276). "Reports of
Assistant Commissioners of the Freedmen's Bureau." 1866.
40th Congress, 1st session:
Senate Executive Document No. 1 (serial 1308). "Letter of
the Secretary of War." 1868.

In addition to the reports of the House and Senate, a variety
of other documents issued under the authority of the federal
government were used. The more important of these were the
following: *The War of the Rebellion: A Compilation of the Official Records of the Union and Confederate Armies* (128 vols.,
Washington, 1880-1901); Bureau of the Census, *Negro Population, 1790-1915* (Washington, 1918); Commissioner of Agriculture, *Report for the Year 1866* (Washington, 1867) and *Report
for the Year 1870* (Washington, 1871); Department of the Interior, *Report of the Commissioner of Education: Common
Schools in South Carolina, 1863-1900* (2 vols., Washington, 1906);
*Report of the Joint Select Committee to Inquire into the Condi-
tion of Affairs in the Late Insurrectionary States* (13 vols., Washington, 1872); Amory D. Mayo, "The Work of Certain Northern
Churches in the Education of the Freedmen, 1861-1900," *Report
of the Commissioner of Education for the Year 1902,* I (Washington, 1903); Julius H. Parmelee, "Freedmen's Aid Societies, 1861-
1871," Bureau of Education, *Bulletin 38* (Washington, 1917).

PERIODICAL LITERATURE

Of the various historical journals concerned with Southern
history, the *Journal of Negro History* proved most helpful for
this study. The following from its files were unusually valuable:
Herbert Aptheker, "South Carolina Negro Conventions, 1865,"
XXXI (1946), 91-97; G. K. Eggleston, "The Work of the Relief
Societies During the Civil War," XIV (1929), 272-99; Luther P.

Jackson, "The Educational Efforts of the Freedmen's Bureau and the Freedmen's Aid Societies in South Carolina, 1862-1872," VIII (1923), 1-40; Robert H. Woody, "Jonathan Jasper Wright, Associate Justice of the Supreme Court of South Carolina, 1870-1877," XVIII (1933), 114-31; Monroe Work, "Some Negro Members of Reconstruction Conventions and Legislatures and of Congress," V (1920), 63-119; A. A. Taylor, "The Negro in South Carolina During Reconstruction," IX (1924), 241-364, 381-569.

The *Journal of Southern History* also contained several articles that yielded useful information. Principal among them were these: Paul W. Gates, "Federal Land Policy in the South, 1866-1868," VI (1940), 303-30; John and La Wanda Cox, "General O. O. Howard and the 'Misrepresented Bureau,'" XIX (1953), 427-56; Elizabeth Bethel, "The Freedmen's Bureau in Alabama," XIV (1948), 49-92; Henry L. Swint, "Northern Interest in the Shoeless Southerner," XVI (1950), 457-71.

Articles located in various other journals were also used with profit. Chief among them were the following: La Wanda Cox, "The Promise of Land for the Freedmen," *Mississippi Valley Historical Review*, XLV (1958), 413-40; Henry L. Swint (ed.), "Reports from Educational Agents of the Freedmen's Bureau in Tennessee, 1865-1870," *Tennessee Historical Quarterly*, I (1942), 51-80, 152-70; Willis D. Boyd, "Negro Colonization in the Reconstruction Era, 1865-1870," *Georgia Historical Quarterly*, XL (1956), 360-82; J. G. Randall, "Some Legal Aspects of the Confiscation Acts of the Civil War," *American Historical Review*, XVIII (1912), 79-96, and, in the same journal, "Captured and Abandoned Property During the Civil War," XIX (1913), 65-79; Robert H. Woody, "Franklin J. Moses, Jr., Scalawag Governor of South Carolina, 1872-1874," *North Carolina Historical Review*, X (1933), 111-32, and "The Labor and Immigration Problem of South Carolina During Reconstruction," *Mississippi Valley Historical Review*, XVIII (1931), 195-212; Elizabeth G. Rice, "A Yankee Teacher in the South," *Century Magazine*, LXII (1901), 151-54; Edgar W. Knight, "Reconstruction and Education in South Carolina," *South Atlantic Quarterly*, XVIII (1919), 350-61; E. L. Pierce, "The Freedmen at Port Royal," *Atlantic Monthly*, XII (1863), 291-315; W. E. B. DuBois, "The Freedmen's Bureau," *Atlantic Monthly*, LXXXVII (1901), 354-65; Harriet Beecher Stowe, "The Education of the Freedmen," *North American Re-*

view, CXXVIII (1879), 605-15; "The Future of the Freedmen," *Southern Presbyterian Review,* XIX (1868), 286-90; and two unsigned articles from the *North American Review:* "The Freedmen at Port Royal," CI (1865), 1-28, and "Education of the Freedmen," CI (1865), 528-49.

Two periodicals of a literary and political nature that devoted considerable attention to affairs in the South were: *Harper's Weekly: A Journal of Civilization* and *The Nation.* The columns of the latter were especially rewarding for this study.

Although not directly useful for this study, several articles that relate the history of the Bureau in other states are interesting for the comparison they offer with the agency's operations in South Carolina. They are the following: William T. Alderson, Jr., "The Freedmen's Bureau and Negro Education in Virginia," *North Carolina Historical Review,* XXIX (1952), 64-90; Claude Elliott, "The Freedmen's Bureau in Texas," *Southwestern Historical Quarterly,* LVI (1948), 1-24; John C. Engelsman, "The Freedmen's Bureau in Louisiana," *Louisiana Historical Quarterly,* XXXII (1949), 145-224; Weymouth Jordan, "The Freedmen's Bureau in Tennessee," *East Tennessee Historical Society Publications,* No. 11 (1939), 47-61; J. G. de Roulhac Hamilton, "The Freedmen's Bureau in North Carolina," *South Atlantic Quarterly,* VIII (1909), 53-67, 154-63; W. A. Lowe, "The Freedmen's Bureau and Civil Rights in Maryland," *Journal of Negro History,* XXXVII (1952), 221-76.

DIARIES, LETTERS, MEMOIRS, AND TRAVEL ACCOUNTS

Drawn from the experience of the writers and providing a first-hand feeling that no subsequent secondary work can convey are the numerous published letters and diaries of contemporaries. Outstanding in this respect were the following: Rupert S. Holland (ed.), *Letters and Diary of Laura M. Towne, Written from the Sea Islands of South Carolina, 1862-1884* (Cambridge, 1912), a work which is invaluable for its description of the sea island life of the Negroes; Mary Ames, *From a New England Woman's Diary in Dixie in 1865* (Springfield, 1906), helpful for the material it contains about the progress in schooling for the freedmen; Ray Allen Billington (ed.), *The Journal of Charlotte L. Forten*

(New York, 1953), revealing the reaction of a Negro teacher among her own people of the day; Elizabeth Ware Pearson (ed.), *Letters from Port Royal, Written at the Time of the Civil War* (Boston, 1906), containing a wealth of information about the conditions of freed labor in the region; and Henrietta S. Jaquette (ed.), *South After Gettysburg: Letters of Cornelia Hancock, 1863-1868* (New York, 1956), the story of a Quaker teacher who began the Laing School for Negroes in Mt. Pleasant in 1866.

Several other works shed light upon conditions in the state in the immediate post-war period: Arney R. Childs (ed.), *The Private Journal of William Henry Ravenel, 1859-1887* (Columbia, 1947); J. H. Easterby (ed.), *The South Carolina Rice Plantation as Revealed in the Papers of Robert F. W. Allston* (Chicago, 1945); Daniel E. H. Smith and others (eds.), *Mason Smith Family Letters, 1860-1868* (Columbia, 1950); Mary Boykin Chesnut, *A Diary from Dixie*, ed. Ben Ames Williams (Boston, 1950); J. W. Alvord, *Letters from the South Relating to the Condition of the Freedmen* (9 vols., Washington, 1870), a collection especially useful for comments upon the Bureau's educational program.

Of the great number and variety of memoirs and reminiscences by contemporaries, several were especially useful: Elizabeth H. Botume, *First Days Among the Contrabands* (Boston, 1893); Elizabeth Allen Coxe, *Memories of a South Carolina Plantation During the War* (Philadelphia, 1912); Rossa B. Cooley, *School Acres: An Adventure in Rural Education* (New Haven, 1930); William D. Armes (ed.), *The Autobiography of Joseph Le Conte* (New York, 1903); D. E. Huger Smith, *A Charlestonian's Recollections, 1846-1913* (Charleston, 1950); Carl Schurz, *Reminiscences* (3 vols., New York, 1908); Sara F. Hughes (ed.), *Letters and Recollections of John Murray Forbes* (2 vols., Boston, 1940); A. Toomer Porter, *Led On! Step by Step; Scenes from . . . Life in the South, 1828-1898: An Autobiography* (New York, 1899); Richard Lathers, *Reminiscences: Sixty Years of a Busy Life in South Carolina, Massachusetts, and New York* (New York, 1907); Edwin J. Scott, *Random Recollections of a Long Life, 1806 to 1876* (Columbia, 1884).

Two works which are very helpful in revealing the native white disdain toward the Bureau are Edward L. Wells, *Hampton and Reconstruction* (Columbia, 1907), a work which vigorously condemns the whole reconstruction program of the Radicals, and John A. Leland, *A Voice from South Carolina, Twelve Chapters Before Hampton, Two Chapters After Hampton* (Charleston, 1879), a narrative which is rancorous in its attitude towards the Bureau.

Three works which were of more than ordinary value and thus deserve special mention are these: John W. De Forest, *A Union Officer in Reconstruction*, ed. James F. Croushore and David M. Potter (New Haven, 1948); De Forest was a careful, perceptive, and articulate observer who saw the good as well as the bad of the society about him, and who saw with a rare detachment both the potential and the limitations of the Bureau. The *Autobiography of Oliver O. Howard* (2 vols., New York, 1906) is a work shedding light on many phases of the Bureau's work and also revealing some useful information about some of the episodes bearing upon the history of the agency in South Carolina. Another work which was of considerable usefulness was Benjamin F. Perry, *Reminiscences of Public Men, with Speeches and Addresses* (2nd series, Greenville, 1889), the memoir of a longtime political leader in the state who served as provisional governor in 1865.

Numerous travelers from the North and from abroad visited the state and recorded their impressions during the Reconstruction era. The accounts of most Northern observers suffer from an obvious bias towards the South, and those of most foreign travelers from a superficiality as a result of the brevity and speed of their visit. Nevertheless, these travel accounts, if used with discretion, constitute an important source for understanding the events as well as the temper of the times. Most valuable for this study were Sidney Andrews, *The South Since the War, as Shown by Fourteen Weeks of Travel and Observation in Georgia and the Carolinas* (Boston, 1866), a work of exceptional merit as a travel account; J. T. Trowbridge, *The South: A Tour of Its Battle-Fields and Ruined Cities, A Journey Through the Desolated States* (Hartford, 1866), especially useful for the light it sheds on the question of free labor; and David Macrae, *The Americans at Home* (New York, 1952), an account of objectivity and perception that makes one wish the author had had more time at his disposal.

Other travel accounts that proved useful in varying degrees

are these: Henry E. Tremain, *Two Days of War: A Gettysburg Narrative and Other Excursions* (New York, 1905); F. Barham Zincke, *Last Winter in the United States; Being Table Talk Collected During a Tour Through the Southern Confederation, the Far West, the Rocky Mountains, Etc.* (London, 1868); Whitelaw Reid, *After the War: A Southern Tour, May 1, 1865-May 1, 1866* (New York, 1866); Henry Latham, *Black and White: A Journal Of Three Months' Tour in the United States* (London, 1867); John H. Kennaway, *On Sherman's Track, or the South After the War* (London, 1867); George Rose, *The Great Country, or Impressions of America* (London, 1868).

BIOGRAPHIES

The Dictionary of American Biography, edited by Allen Johnson and Dumas Malone (20 vols., supplements and index, 1927-1958), is the standard biographical reference work. Also helpful for the attention it gives to individuals later obscured by the course of time is *Appleton's Cyclopaedia of American Biography* (6 vols., 1887-1889). Full-length biographies of individuals who were prominent either in the Bureau or in state affairs of the period are few. Of these, the following afforded some useful information: Frank A. Rollin, *Life and Public Services of Martin R. Delany* (Boston, 1883); Matilda Evans, *Martha Schofield: Pioneer Negro Educator* (Columbia, 1916); Lillian Kibler, *Benjamin F. Perry: South Carolina Unionist* (Durham, 1946); Henry D. Capers, *The Life and Times of C. G. Memminger* (Richmond, 1893); Mary D. O'Connor, *The Life and Letters of M. O. O'Connor* (New York, 1893); Leroy F. Youmans, *Sketch of the Life of Governor Andrew Gordon Magrath* (Charleston, 1896).

GENERAL AND SPECIAL STUDIES

Within the last generation scholars have produced a great number and variety of works dealing with Reconstruction in one or another of its many phases. Not all are concerned with the Bureau directly, but the following need to be consulted to appreciate the setting within which the institution sought to achieve its goal. The most recent, though not necessarily the best, study of the Reconstruction era is Kenneth Stampp, *The Era of Reconstruction* (New York, 1965). An excellent short account, with a very useful bibliography appended, is John Hope Franklin, *Reconstruction: After the Civil War* (Chicago, 1961); the same author's *From Slavery to Freedom: A History of American Negroes* (New York, 1956, 2nd ed.) is a work of uncommon merit. Among the older works, many of whose judgments have been altered by recent scholarship, are three that can still be used with profit: William Archibald Dunning, *Reconstruction, Political, and Economic, 1865-1877* (New York, 1907); John W. Burgess, *Reconstruction and the Constitution, 1866-1876* (New York, 1907); and Walter L. Fleming, *The Sequel of Appomattox* (New Haven, 1919). Also old but still very useful are two collections of documents: Edward McPherson, *The Political History of the United States of America During the Period of Reconstruction* (Washington, 1871), and Walter L. Fleming (ed.), *Documentary History of Reconstruction: Political, Military, Social, Religious, Educational, and Industrial* (2 vols., Cleveland, 1906-7). A more recent documentary collection is Herbert Aptheker, *A Documentary History of the Negro People in the United States* (New York, 1951).

Within the last thirty years have appeared a large number of general and special studies on Reconstruction. A good introduction to the period, and a work with a superb bibliography, is J. G. Randall and David Donald, *The Civil War and Reconstruction* (Boston, 1961, 2nd ed.). Among the better of the recent studies are the following: Paul H. Buck, *The Road to Reunion, 1865-1900* (Boston, 1937); George F. Milton, *The Age of Hate: Andrew Johnson and the Radicals* (New York, 1930), though Milton's book ought to be balanced against Eric McKitrick, *Andrew Johnson and Reconstruction* (Chicago, 1960); W. E. B. Du Bois, *Black Reconstruction* (New York, 1935); and E. Merton Coulter, *The South During Reconstruction, 1865-1877* (Baton Rouge, 1947), a work which does not accept the revisionist point of view about the era. Of some help is Henderson H. Donald, *The Negro Freedman: Life Conditions of the American Negro in the Early Years After Emancipation* (New York, 1952), though the author too readily offers evidence disparaging to the freedmen.

Of the large number of special studies, the following proved to be useful in varying degrees: Horace M. Bond, *The Education of the Negro in the American Social Order* (New York, 1934); J. L. M. Curry, *Peabody Education Fund: A Brief Sketch of George Peabody and A History of the Peabody Education Fund Through Thirty Years* (Cambridge, 1898); Edgar W. Knight, *The Influence of Reconstruction on Education in the South* (New York, 1913); Walter L. Fleming, *The Freedmen's Savings Bank: A Chapter in the Economic History of the Negro Race* (Chapel Hill, 1927); John P. Hollis, *The Early Period of Reconstruction in South Carolina* (Baltimore, 1905); Anne M. Holmes, *The New York Ladies Southern Relief Association, 1866-1867* (New York, 1926); Guion G. Johnson, *A Social History of the Sea Islands, with Special Reference to St. Helena, South Carolina* (Chapel Hill, 1930); J. G. Randall, *Constitutional Problems Under Lincoln* (Urbana, 1951, rev. ed.); Henry L. Swint, *The Northern Teacher in the South, 1862-1870* (Nashville, 1941); Alrutheus A. Taylor, *The Negro in South Carolina During Reconstruction* (Washington, 1924); John F. Thomason, *Foundations of the Public Schools of South Carolina* (Columbia, 1925); Otis Singletary, *Negro Militia and Reconstruction* (Austin, 1957); Ralph Morrow, *Northern Methodism and Reconstruction* (East Lansing, 1956); George B. Tindall, *South Carolina Negroes, 1877-1900* (Columbia, 1952); Charles H. Wesley, *Negro Labor in the United States, 1850-1925* (New York, 1927); Bell I. Wiley, *Southern Negroes, 1861-1865* (New Haven, 1938). Appearing too late for use in this study is an excellent work by Joel Williamson, *After Slavery: The Negro in South Carolina During Reconstruction, 1861-1877* (Chapel Hill, 1965).

Four other works deserve special recognition for their usefulness to this study. The first is Francis B. Simkins and Robert H. Woody, *South Carolina During Reconstruction* (Chapel Hill, 1932). This is the indispensable work for any student in studying the era of Reconstruction in the state; it is in many ways a model work, with its high caliber of scholarship, of objectivity, of comprehensiveness, and of literary merit. The second is George R. Bentley, *A History of the Freedmen's Bureau* (Philadelphia, 1955), a work which supplants the older and more limited study of Paul S. Peirce, *The Freedmen's Bureau, A Chapter in the History of Reconstruction* (Iowa City, 1904). Bentley's book has a scholarly range and depth that makes it, in all probability, the definitive work on the history of the Bureau at the national level; my study does not agree in all respects with his judgments, but I am indebted to him both for many points of substance and several sources which otherwise may not have been used. Another work deserving special mention is the fifty-year-old monograph of Laura Josephine Webster, *The Operation of the Freedmen's Bureau in South Carolina* (Northampton, 1916). Severely limited by the fact that the Bureau Records were still not open for investigation at the time of its writing, the work, nevertheless, proved helpful as an introduction to the subject and as a guide to important government publications. Finally, Willie Lee Rose, *Rehearsal for Reconstruction: The Port Royal Experiment* (Indianapolis, 1964) is a work of uncommon merit in its portrayal of the wartime effort to move the Negroes of the region along the road from bondage to freedom.

restored, 55-56; disapproves creation of Bureau courts, 103; vetoes Freedmen's Bureau bill, 133-34

K

Ketchum, A. P., role in sea island controversy, 58-60

L

Labor of Negroes. *See* Contract labor
Land for freedmen, set apart by Sherman, 8; given by "possessory titles," 8; assigned to Bureau, 53; distributed by Bureau, 55-56; returned to white owners, 56-57. *See also* Abandoned lands, Sea Islands
Leslie, C. P., 26
Lincoln, Abraham, issues Emancipation Proclamation, 3

M

Marriage regulations, of freedmen, established by Bureau, 105-6; defined by state legislature, 107; effect upon Negro families, 108
Mather, Rachel, 83
Medical program of Bureau, organized, 48; amount of aid given under, 48-50. *See also* Relief administered by Bureau
Military forces, in S.C., conflict with Bureau, 12-15, 100, 132; personnel assigned to Bureau duty, 26; role in solving sea island controversy, 61; role in developing contract labor system, 67-68
Monroe, Abby D., 83
Morris Street School, 94

N

Neide, Horace, 22
New England Freedmen's Commission, 84

O

Orr, James L., elected governor, 29-30; concern over widespread destitution, 40-43; on contract labor system, 80; protests actions of Bureau agents, 118

P

Parker, Niles G., 26
Penn School Number One, 92
Perry, Benjamin F., named provisional governor, 29; reaches agreement with military concerning judicial authority over freedmen, 100
Pickens, F. W., 66
Pierce, E. L., proposes organization of Sea Island Experiment, 5
Pillsbury, Gilbert, 33
Porter, A. Toomer, 92
Private societies, Northern, aid in Southern relief, 43; role in supporting Negro education, 84-85; rivalry among, 86; declining support of Negro education, 89
Provost Courts, assume jurisdiction over legal rights of freedmen, 100-1

R

Radicals, launch reconstruction plan, 30-31
Reconstruction. *See* Radicals, South Carolina
Refugees, white, relief given to, 40-41
Reid, Whitelaw, tours South, 9, 128
Relief administered by Bureau, with military co-operation, 14-15; amount of, 38-39, 41, 43-44; definition of ration, 38n; evaluation of program, 50-51; program condemned by white Southerners, 120-21

S

Saxton, Rufus, named director of Sea Island Experiment, 6; named assistant commissioner of Bureau, 9; early life and character, 9-10, 116; proposes bill broadening Bureau power, 10-11; reluctance to carry out presidential land policy, 12; compelled to reduce Bureau personnel, 12; major problems in organizing Bureau, 13-15; removed as assistant commissioner, 16; evaluation of work, 16; criticized by Steedman-Fullerton investigation, 28; organizes relief program,